The Invisible Edge

WHAT FUELS YOUR SUCCESS MIGHT BE WHAT LIMITS IT

by *Angela Belford*

The Invisible Edge by Angela Belford
Published by Be Freaking Awesome, LLC
PO Box 1851, Fayetteville, AR 72702
www.BFreakingAwesome.com

Book Design, Layout and Cover by Micah Bland, Elizabeth
Kirkendall, and Raylee Knight; editing by Erica Ord at The
Belford Group. Author Photo by Nidhi Dahiya of Nids Creations

ISBN: 978-0-9991862-4-4
For information about special discounts available for bulk
purchases, sales promotions, fund-raising and educational
needs, contact Be Freaking Awesome, LLC at
479.443.9945 or hello@BFreakingAwesome.com.

Contents

Dedicated To

Barry Belford
So many miles have connected our hearts.
I love you and appreciate every version of you.

Sami, Josh, and Lexi
If I would have known how awesome adults kids
would be I would have had so many more.
You are my greatest blessing.

Chris and Abby
You chose this family and I'm forever grateful.
I hope we bring you as much love as you bring us.

Henry, Peter, and Maxine
It is true my favorite people call me Lala.
You are the hope for tomorrow and the joy of
today.

A Note from Angela

This book started as a hunch.

I had spent years sitting across from accomplished people, people who had built real things, led real teams, made real sacrifices, and were still hitting a ceiling they could not explain. They had done the work. Read the books. Hired the consultants. And something was still in the way.

The hunch was this: the thing stopping them was not a skill gap. It was a belief. One planted long before they ever stepped into the role they were in now. A belief that had powered their climb and was quietly, invisibly, becoming their ceiling. The fuel that got them here could not get them there.

I started coaching with that hypothesis and paid close attention. Over several years and more than forty clients, the pattern held. It showed up in family businesses navigating transitions, in executives who had earned every credential and still doubted their right to lead, in entrepreneurs who had built something real and could not figure out why the next level felt so hard. Different industries. Different wounds. The same invisible edge.

When Traveling Light came out, readers kept telling me the same thing: it was not a book you could just sit down and consume. It was a big juicy steak. Good, but you had to take it slow. You had to sit with it. I heard that as a gift and as an invitation. Some people need the framework first. Others need the story first, something they can live inside before they are ready to do the work.

So I designed five characters. I wrote the early bones of their sessions. And then I put the manuscript aside and went back to the coaching room, because the book was not ready and neither was I.

The last stretch of writing is where everything crystallized. Not because I finally found the right structure, but because I had finally sat with enough people, long enough, to know what was true.

Every book I have written has been shaped by other people. My first two books went through editors I paid thousands of dollars to help me find the structure, tighten the language, and make the manuscript into something a reader could actually hold. Each time, my biggest job in that process was making sure it still sounded like me when we were done.

This book was no different, except the tools were different. I used AI in the process. ChatGPT helped me develop the characters and their backstories in the early stages. Claude was in the editing room with me for months, drawing on hundreds of hours of real coaching transcripts to help match my voice and work through the structure. Same job I have always hired for. Different century.

And the same challenge: making sure it still sounded like me when we were done.

Those tools worked because I came in with something real. My methodology. My voice. My understanding of how these patterns actually live in the body. The AI could mirror back what I already knew. It could not know it for me. The line-by-line editing, the does-this-character-ring-true work, that part was mine. The tools were a scaffold. The building is mine.

I also want to name Shannon McNeill-Sawney, membership director at the Fayetteville Chamber of Commerce, who makes intentional feel natural in every room she is in. She appears briefly in these pages because she belongs in them.

This is my third book. It is the first one I felt proud of while I was still writing it.

If you have made it to this page, I want to ask you something. Not a rhetorical question. A real one.

What have you been running on?

Not what you tell people at dinner. Not the story that sounds good. The actual fuel. The belief that has been underneath all of it, powering the climb, the one you have never quite looked at directly.

That is where the work starts. And if this book did its job, you already know what it is.

Angela

A NOTE ON THE CHARACTERS

The people you'll meet in these pages are entirely fictional. Julia, Roman, Cameron, Theodore, Jade, and Emily are composites drawn from years of coaching work, conversations, and the universal patterns that show up when human beings get honest about what's holding them back.

Any resemblance to specific people, living or dead, is coincidental. These characters are not portraits of any individual client, colleague, or person in my life. They are, in the truest sense, invented.

That said, their struggles are real. The beliefs they carry, the ways those beliefs quietly shape every decision, the moment something finally shifts: those I've witnessed dozens of times. If you see yourself somewhere in these pages, that's not an accident. It just means you're human.

CHAPTER 1

Roman Hale, Hale & Co. Architects

Roman Hale stood at the head of the conference table while the leadership team of Hale & Co. Architects reviewed the proposal in front of them.

No one spoke. Pages turned quietly around the table as the senior leadership team studied the numbers, projections, and organizational charts outlining what the next twelve months could look like if Roman made one decision.

Through the tall windows behind them, the city stretched outward in clean lines of glass and steel. Roman had always appreciated that about architecture. Structure meant predictability. If the calculations were correct, the building stood.

Across the center of the table sat a thin leather folder.

Inside it was the future of Hale & Co.

Or its collapse.

Three years earlier, Roman had inherited the firm after his father died without warning. There had been no transition plan, no gradual handoff, just a funeral and a leadership team suddenly looking to him for direction the following Monday morning.

His goal then had been simple.

Stabilize.

And he had done it. Actually, more than just stabilize. The firm was more profitable than ever. Projects were steady. Clients remained loyal. Forty-two employees continued doing the work his father had spent decades building.

On paper, everything looked solid.

Which was why the proposal on the table felt heavier than it should have.

Across from him, David Mercer closed the folder in front of him and leaned back in his chair.

As Director of Operations, Mercer had spent nearly twenty years inside the firm. He had worked under Roman's father long before Roman joined full-time, and he carried the quiet authority of someone who knew exactly how the place ran.

"You're serious about this?" Mercer asked.

Roman nodded once. "I wouldn't have brought it to this room if I weren't."

Mercer tapped the folder with two fingers. "Acquiring another firm isn't a small adjustment."

"I'm aware."

Inside the proposal were the details for Ellison & Wright Architects, a boutique firm in the next county with a strong reputation and a founder ready to retire. Thirty years of carefully built client relationships. Twelve employees. A portfolio of respected work.

And no successor.

Two weeks earlier, the founder had asked Roman to meet him for coffee.

The conversation had been brief and direct.

"I'm not selling to a corporate group," the man said. "They'll rebrand the place and strip out everything that made it work."

Roman understood.

The man studied him for a moment before continuing. "I built this firm carefully. I'd like it to stay that way."

Then he said the sentence Roman hadn't stopped thinking about since.

"You're the only one I'd trust with it."

At the time, Roman had taken it as a sign of respect.

Now it felt more like responsibility.

Mercer slid the proposal back to the center of the table.

"If we move forward," he said, "we double our staff overnight."

"Yes."

"We inherit their projects."

"Yes."

"Their culture."

Roman held his gaze steady. "Yes."

Mercer folded his hands together. "That's a lot of moving parts."

Roman didn't disagree.

Architects were trained to design systems behaving predictably. Foundations distributed weight. Steel beams carried load. Structural calculations left little room for guesswork.

Acquisitions worked differently.

Acquisitions introduced variables.

Across the table, one of the senior principals spoke.

"What's your recommendation?"

Roman had prepared for the question.

He had reviewed the financial projections twice. He had studied their staffing structure, their contracts, and the potential overlap between the firms. He had mapped out possible integration scenarios and identified the risks.

Still, the moment stretched longer than he intended.

His mind moved through the possibilities like layered blueprints.

Staff integration. Cash flow exposure. Leadership transitions.

Forty-two employees are depending on him to get this right. Again.

His father had made decisions like this quickly. Cleanly. Roman remembered standing beside him on job sites as a teenager while contractors debated structural adjustments. His father would listen, ask two precise questions, and decide.

No hesitation.

The room waited. Roman felt the pause clearly, the familiar moment when his thoughts stopped moving forward and began circling. He straightened slightly.

"My recommendation," he said finally, "is that we continue due diligence before making a final decision."

No one looked surprised. Mercer nodded. "Seems reasonable."

Reasonable. Responsible. Safe.

None of which sounded anything like the kind of leader his father had been.

The meeting ended shortly afterward. One by one, the leadership team gathered their papers and left the room. Roman remained where he was, looking out at the city.

Behind him, one of the associates, Jim, paused near the door.

"Roman."

Roman turned.

Jim hesitated, like he was deciding whether to say the next thing. "You're speaking at the Chamber development event next month, right?"

Roman nodded.

"My wife worked with a speaking coach before a big investor presentation last year." He shrugged. "Said it changed how she showed up in the room." He glanced at his phone briefly. "Emily Carter. Just thought of it."

He slipped his phone back into his pocket and left.

Roman turned back to the windows.

The city sat still and ordered beyond the glass. Forty-two employees. Twelve more if he moved forward. A founder who had trusted him with thirty years of careful work.

He picked up the leather folder from the table and held it for a moment.

In architecture, a structure failed when the load exceeded its capacity. The calculation was straightforward. You knew the variables. You ran the numbers. You either built it or you didn't.

He had inherited the firm his father built.

What he hadn't inherited was certainty.

Roman walked back to his office, the folder under his arm. The city sat quiet beyond the glass. and offering nothing back.

•   •   •

Across town, Julia Ross was staring at a bakery oven and wondering if she had built something that was already falling apart.

CHAPTER 2

Julia Ross, The French Bakery

The bakery smelled like butter and cardamom long before the sun came up.

Julia stood at the stainless steel counter shaping dough while the first batch of brioche proofed beside the ovens. Outside, the streetlights still cast soft pools of yellow across the quiet sidewalk. This hour was her favorite. No customers. No decisions. Just flour and warmth with the steady hum of the ovens in the background.

She pressed the heel of her hand into the dough and folded it back.

Chef Renee had taught her to knead this way. Not family. Not culinary school. Chef Renee ran the morning station at a campus bakery with the kind of calm you only get when you stop trying to impress anyone. Julia had been nineteen. She took the weekend shifts because she needed the money. She stayed because she liked who she was in that kitchen.

She had spent three years after culinary school moving through other kitchens, learning what she liked and what she didn't, before she landed at The French Bakery. Henri had been running it for twenty-two years by then, a small corner shop two blocks from what would eventually become a very different neighborhood. He was meticulous about dough and completely indifferent to branding.

He had named the place The French Bakery because, he explained without apology, it was a bakery, and he was French. Julia had found this so purely him that she never once considered changing the name.

She had worked alongside Henri for three years before he called her into the back office one afternoon, set a folder on the table between them, and told her his brother had a place in Florida with a spare room and a fishing boat, and that was where he intended to be by spring. He had already spoken to his accountant. He thought she should have the first right of refusal.

She had said yes before he finished the sentence.

That had been seven years ago. She scraped together everything she had, borrowed the rest, and signed the papers on a Tuesday morning with shaking hands and a certainty she still couldn't fully explain. Henri flew to Tampa in March. He sent a postcard that June with a photo of a redfish and three words: beautiful down here. She taped it inside the cabinet above the espresso machine. Sun-faded now, the fish barely visible.

The morning after he left, she had stood alone in the kitchen at four-thirty and understood for the first time what she had taken on.

She slid the tray into the proofing cabinet and leaned back against the counter. The digital clock on the wall read 6:18 AM. Two hours until the morning rush.

She glanced toward the small office at the back of the shop. Through the open door, she could see the desk, the scheduling board on the wall covered in her handwriting, the second chair that had never quite found a reason to leave. Marcus had picked it out. He had strong opinions about office chairs, about inventory systems, about the particular software that would make the business side of things manageable for someone whose brain worked the way Julia's did. He had spreadsheets for things she hadn't known needed spreadsheets.

She looked away.

The display cases along the front wall sat empty, their glass polished and waiting. Later, they would hold croissants, fruit tarts, cinnamon rolls, and the lavender shortbread that regulars drove across town to buy. But at this moment, the bakery looked like a stage before the performance. Quiet and expectant.

She slid the tray into the proofing cabinet and leaned back against the counter. In two hours, the morning rush would begin, and the cases would fill, and by nine o'clock, the lavender shortbread would be gone, just as every day. The standing order from the law firm on Fifth had been on the books for four years. The older gentleman who came in every Tuesday for a plain croissant and stayed for twenty minutes had been coming since Henri's time. Last week, a woman had driven forty minutes because her daughter had mentioned the cardamom brioche at a dinner party.

The French Bakery was good. Julia knew it was good.

She reached for her phone and opened the sales dashboard she had promised herself she would check every morning.

The numbers appeared on the screen, and she exhaled slowly. Two locations. Double the overhead, double the staffing, double the...felt like everything. Not terrible. But not strong enough to relax either. That had become the rhythm of the past year: good enough to stay open, not good enough to breathe.

A new bakery had opened two blocks away six months ago. Sleek branding, a carefully chosen name, a pastry chef who posted elaborate desserts on social media every morning before sunrise. Their croissants were laminated to perfection. Their Instagram following was larger than Julia's monthly foot traffic. The owners looked about twenty-four.

She turned the phone face down on the counter.

Comparison was a dangerous way to start the day. Still, the thought returned the way it often did.

Maybe I'm just not built for this level anymore.

She wiped flour from her hands and crossed the kitchen to start the espresso machine. Steam hissed to life. The ritual steadied her slightly.

Marcus had quit his job at the logistics firm two years after she bought the bakery, walked in one morning with coffee and a spreadsheet, and said he wanted to help build something actually theirs. For four years, he had been the other half of the operation, the part who understood margins, supplier contracts, and what she couldn't track on her own.

They had talked about expanding, and then they had actually done it. Two years before he left, Marcus found a second location three miles away, negotiated the lease, and built the infrastructure to replicate what they had built at Henri's original space. Julia developed the menu, trained the kitchen staff, and made it feel like The French Bakery rather than a copy of it.

Then a college roommate called from San Francisco.

The offer wouldn't come along twice, Marcus said. He wanted her to come. Had framed it carefully the first time, more directly the second, then with a kind of exhausted honesty the third. She still thought about it sometimes when the shop was very quiet. The French Bakery had been open for six years by then. She had chosen it once already.

She stayed.

When he left, he took the business plan she had never written down because she hadn't needed to. It had lived in the space between them. Both locations were still hers. The original felt like home. The second was harder to be in. She showed up twice a week and did what needed doing. She had not changed anything he built, partly because it worked, and partly because changing it felt like something she was not ready to name.

• • •

She almost didn't go.

The Chamber after-hours had been on her calendar for three weeks, and she had spent most of the drive over composing reasons to turn around. She arrived twelve minutes late, took a glass of wine she didn't really want, and positioned herself near the back of the room, where the lighting was forgiving, and the exit was close.

The room was full of people who seemed to know exactly why they were there. Name tags and easy laughter, and the particular energy of people who found rooms like this energizing rather than exhausting. Julia smiled at two people who made eye contact and then found reasons to look at their phones.

She was calculating how soon she could leave without it being obvious when Shannon moved to the front of the room.

Shannon had taken over the Chamber membership a couple of years ago and had quietly changed the temperature of the room. Julia had noticed it happening, the way events started feeling less like obligation and more like something worth showing up for. Shannon had a gift for making the intentional feel natural, as if the structure were invisible and the connection was the only thing.

"We network with intention here," Shannon said, which she said at every event and somehow meant every time. She turned first to the newer faces in the room, inviting each to introduce themselves, then moved through the group herself to make sure people found their way over. Twenty minutes later, she gathered the ambassadors, each introduction brief and warm, in a way that felt like Shannon's influence rather than a script.

"Before we open the floor," Shannon said, "I want to give a quick minute to someone I've been wanting you all to hear from. Emily Carter works with business owners in this community, and she said something to me last month that I haven't stopped thinking about." She smiled. "Emily, go ahead."

A woman near the front turned to face the room. No notes. No slide deck. Nothing to hold. Her presence was more convincing than performance.

"I was at an event a lot like this one about ten years ago," Emily said. "Standing about where most of you are standing. And I realized I had been at that same spot, physically, at about a dozen events before that one. Near the back. Near the door." A few quiet laughs. "Not because I didn't want to connect. Because I had a story running that said the people in the front of the room had something I didn't. And until I figured out what that story was, I kept ending up in the same spot."

She paused, looked around the room thoughtfully.

"Most of us walk in here with that story already going. About whether we belong. Whether we have something worth saying. Whether anyone actually wants to hear it. I work with business owners on what's underneath that. Because until you can see it, it runs everything. Your decisions. Your growth. Even where you stand at a networking event."

She smiled, warm and unhurried. "That's all. Go network with intention."

Shannon laughed, and the room shifted back into motion.

Julia didn't move for a moment.

Then she finished her wine, set the glass down, and made her way toward the front of the room.

Emily was already in conversation with someone, relaxed and genuinely engaged. Julia waited, which was not something she usually did at events like this. As the conversation wrapped up, Julia heard Emily say, "You said your name was Roman, right?" The man nodded. Emily continued, "I hope you give me a call."

When the conversation ended, Emily turned and found her standing there.

"Hi," Julia said. "I own a bakery a few blocks from here. I've been a member for years, and I still end up near the door every time."

Emily smiled. "How long have you had the bakery?"

"Seven years. I bought it from the original owner."

"You beat the statistics," Emily said. "Most independent spots don't see five."

Julia almost said something true. Instead, she said, "Some days it feels like it."

Emily looked at her for a moment with the calm attention of someone who was actually listening. "What kind of days?"

Julia laughed softly, surprised by the question. "The ones where I wonder if I still have what it takes to keep up with what the industry is becoming."

She hadn't planned to say that. She wasn't sure where it came from.

Emily didn't fill the space immediately. She let it land.

"I hear that a lot," she said finally. "More than people expect." She reached into her bag and handed Julia a card. "I run a small mastermind for business owners working through exactly that kind of question. Applications close in a few weeks if it's ever something that feels relevant."

Julia took the card.

She handed Emily one of her own in return, the ones she always carried and rarely gave out.

"The French Bakery," Emily read. She looked up. "I'll come in."

"Henri named it," Julia said. "He was brilliant with dough and terrible with branding."

Emily laughed, genuine and easy. "I like him already."

• • •

A few days later, Julia arrived at the bakery at four-thirty. Same as every day.

She had left Emily's card on her kitchen counter at home, slightly apart from the clutter, in the particular way of things she wasn't ready to deal with and couldn't quite put away. That morning, she had picked it up without deciding to and slipped it into her apron pocket.

Now it sat next to the register, slightly apart from everything else.

She turned it over once in her fingers.

Emily Carter Executive Coach

Underneath, a single line.

Leadership Mastermind – Applications Close Soon

From the kitchen, the timer for the first proof began to beep.

Julia slid the card into the small drawer beneath the register and went back to the dough.

But as she worked, the question followed her like a quiet shadow.

What if the problem isn't the bakery? What if the problem is me?

. . .

Twenty miles north, Cameron Miller was already in the field before sunrise, pushing hard against a question she didn't know how to ask.

CHAPTER 3

Cameron Miller, Miller Farm

The tractor engine rattled across the field as Cameron Miller leaned forward over the steering wheel, scanning the rows ahead of her. Morning fog still held on at the edges of the pasture, and the air smelled like damp soil and cut hay. Her hands rested on the controls, muscle memory doing what her mind had long since stopped tracking.

Three years ago, she had pulled twenty acres from the main rotation and started over. Compacted soil, thin yields, the kind of land that produces because you force it to, rather than because it wants to. Cameron had seen it differently. She mapped a new rotation, sourced the cover crops, and rebuilt the microbial systems in that section. Her father watched from the kitchen window.

The older farmers in the county shook their heads at the expense.

Cameron called it the future.

The land had answered. This season's yields were the strongest the farm had seen in a decade.

The co-op buyer had called twice last month, unprompted. A regional food publication had contacted her about a feature. She had said she'd think about it, which meant she hadn't thought about it at all because there was always something more pressing than talking about herself.

This part she trusted.

Machines made sense. Soil made sense. Rain, drought, and harvest cycles made sense. The land responded to effort.

People were harder.

She cut the engine near the edge of the field and climbed down from the tractor, her boots hitting the dirt with a familiar thud. Across the field, a crew of farmhands was spread across two trucks, loading crates with the efficient rhythm of people who had done it hundreds of times.

Miller's Harvest ran thirty to forty hands on a regular basis, more during planting and harvest seasons. Cameron knew most of them by name, knew which ones cut corners, knew which rows each person was responsible for. She also knew that most of them had stopped asking her questions they already knew the answers to, because asking Cameron meant waiting while she walked over to check herself. Cameron wiped sweat from her forehead with the sleeve of her work shirt and walked toward the nearest truck.

Jake, one of her senior hands, looked up. 'We're short six crates for the co-op order.'

Cameron stopped.

Regenerative farming rebuilt soil, but it didn't rush harvests. Some weeks, the regenerative section produced less while the ground recovered, which threw off the numbers she was trying to reconcile with the rest of the operation.

Again.

Her jaw tightened slightly. "Check the greenhouse row. We may have miscounted the late harvest."

Jake nodded and headed back toward the truck without a word. He had already checked the greenhouse row. She would find out it was his first instinct too, which would not register as information about Jake. It would register as confirmation that she had caught something no one else would have.

Cameron remained where she was for a moment, staring across the field. The land didn't question her. The soil didn't debate her decisions. When something failed, the reason was usually visible. Too much rain, not enough sun, a pest slipping through unnoticed.

Business decisions were different. The moment she stepped into conversations about pricing, distribution, or long-term strategy, something shifted inside her chest. She noticed it every time and filed it under things to push through.

She climbed back onto the tractor and finished the remaining rows, letting the steady rhythm of the work quiet what had started circling in her mind.

By the time she parked near the equipment shed, the morning fog had burned away, and the sun was high over the fields.

Plant. Tend. Harvest.

The pattern had always been simple.

Her phone buzzed in the pocket of her jeans. Cameron pulled it out and glanced at the message from the regional produce buyer.

Need to talk about next week's order. Prices may shift.

Her jaw tightened. Prices had been shifting all year.

The land was improving, and yields were stronger, but getting here had been brutal. Costs rose before profits did. Her father had warned her about that. Margins matter, he had said the day she explained her plan to convert more acreage. He hadn't dismissed her. But he hadn't sounded convinced either.

She slipped the phone back into her pocket and walked toward the barn.

"How many did we finish?" she asked.

"Forty-eight," one of the farmhands replied.

Cameron nodded. Decent. Not great, but decent.

She lifted a crate and carried it toward the truck. One of the farmhands glanced over.

"You good?"

"Yeah," she said.

She always said that. Being tired was acceptable on a farm. Doubt wasn't.

The rest of the afternoon disappeared into the usual rhythm, loading trucks, answering supplier messages, and checking irrigation lines. By the time Cameron finally headed toward the house, the sky had turned a soft orange, meaning the day was almost finished.

Her father was already sitting at the kitchen table with a cup of coffee when she walked in. The television hummed quietly in the background, though neither of them was watching it.

He glanced up. "Long day?"

"Same as usual."

He nodded and took another sip. For a few minutes, they sat in comfortable silence. Cameron had never needed much conversation with him. Their relationship had always been built on shared work more than shared words.

Finally, he said, "Heard the co-op might renegotiate contracts next month."

Cameron pulled out a chair. "Yeah. Got a message about it earlier."

Her father studied her for a moment. "You sure you want to keep pushing the organic conversion this fast?"

The question was calm. Practical. Cameron felt the familiar tightening in her chest, the one she had learned to breathe past.

"I'm sure."

He nodded slowly, his eyes staying on her a moment longer than the conversation required. "I just don't want you carrying more than you have to."

Cameron looked down at the wood grain of the table.

He had farmed this land for forty years. Conventional rows. Predictable fertilizer schedules. Reliable yields. He had built something real, and she respected every inch of it. But she believed the soil could become stronger than it had ever been if she was willing to change how the farm worked.

He wasn't wrong to be cautious. That was the part she never said out loud.

And she wasn't wrong to push. That was the part he never quite said, either.

They finished their coffee without resolving anything, which was how most of their conversations ended. It wasn't distance. It was just the particular language of two people who showed their love by showing up and kept their doubts to themselves.

•   •   •

Later that evening, Cameron stepped out onto the back porch with her laptop. The fields were dark, the rows barely visible beyond the porch light.

She had meant to review the numbers for next week's deliveries. Instead, she found herself on LinkedIn, scrolling without much purpose, the kind of tired where the brain wants distraction but can't commit to anything.

A post caught her eye.

Applications open for the Fall Leadership Mastermind.

She almost kept scrolling.

The description underneath was short. A small group of business owners working through leadership challenges together.

Cameron didn't need a mastermind. She needed a better distribution contract and three more hours in the day.

But something about the phrase leadership challenges made her stop.

The farm wasn't failing. The soil was improving. The crops were strong. The problem wasn't the land.

It was the moment she had to stop working and start deciding.

She clicked the link.

The page opened to a short description and a photo of the facilitator.

Emily Carter. Executive Coach.

Cameron studied the screen for a moment. Then she closed the laptop, went inside, and did not think about it for the rest of the evening.

The next morning, she emailed to schedule a call before she had fully talked herself out of it.

•   •   •

Across town, in a quiet workshop filled with objects from another century, Theodore Sinclair was discovering that certainty was harder to restore than any piece of furniture he had ever touched.

CHAPTER 4

Theodore Sinclair, Art Restorer

Theodore Sinclair stood beneath the workshop light, studying the oil painting mounted on his easel. At first glance, the landscape looked dull and brown, its colors muted beneath a century of yellowed varnish. Most people assumed the painting had simply aged poorly.

Theodore knew better.

He dipped a cotton swab into a small dish of solvent and gently wiped a corner of the canvas. A streak of vibrant blue emerged where the dull film had been removed. Theodore had built a career on what other people overlooked.

He leaned back slightly, examining the small patch he had uncovered. The sky in the painting was far brighter than anyone would have guessed from the surface.

"There you are," he murmured.

He had always liked this moment in the work. The instant when something everyone else believed was faded or ruined revealed it had never needed saving. Just patience..

In the corner of the workshop, his father's lamp cast its familiar circle of light across the workbench. Theodore had moved it once, years ago, repositioning it toward the window to catch the afternoon light differently. It hadn't worked. He had moved it back the same day. Some things had a right place, and you only understood that by disturbing them.

His father had retired twelve years ago, which in practice had meant coming in four days a week instead of five, then three, then two, then whenever something interesting arrived that he wanted to see. The last few years before he passed had been the best years Theodore could remember in the shop. No pressure of ownership between them. Just two men and the work they both loved, moving quietly around each other in a space built for exactly that.

Theodore still reached for the phone sometimes to tell him about a piece.

The bell over the shop door chimed. Theodore glanced up as a man in his thirties stepped inside, holding a small wooden sculpture.

"Hi," the man said. "I found this at my grandmother's house. My mom thought maybe it could be restored."

Theodore stepped forward and accepted the sculpture, turning it carefully in his hands. Hand-carved. Early twentieth century, most likely. The wood had dried slightly, and one corner had cracked, but the craftsmanship was still beautiful.

"Yes," Theodore said. "This can absolutely be restored."

The man nodded politely. "How much would something like that cost?"

The man blinked. "Oh," he said. "That's more than I expected."

Theodore waited.

"I mean," the man continued, shifting the sculpture in his hands, "I could probably just buy something like this online for less."

Theodore nodded calmly. "Yes," he said. "You probably could."

The man hesitated for a moment, suddenly aware of the weight of the sculpture in his hands. "I'll think about it," he said.

"Of course."

The bell chimed again as the door closed behind him. Theodore returned to the workbench and looked back at the painting. For most of his career, people had brought him objects because they believed they were valuable.

Now they brought them because they weren't sure. And more often than not, they left with the same uncertainty.

He lifted the cotton swab again and carefully cleared another small patch of varnish. The colors beneath the surface grew brighter with each stroke. Restoration required patience. The real work was learning to see what still existed beneath the damage before anyone else could.

He was less certain the world still believed it about craftsmanship.

Late in the afternoon, the bell chimed again, but this time the footsteps were familiar.

"Hey, Dad."

Theodore didn't look up immediately. "Done with work already?"

Evan Sinclair set a messenger bag on the counter near the front of the shop. "Client meeting got moved."

Theodore finally glanced up. His son looked exactly as he always did when he stopped by after work, jacket slung over one shoulder, phone still in hand, energy moving faster than the quiet rhythm of the workshop.

Evan wandered over to the painting and studied it for a moment. Then he turned and leaned against the edge of the workbench with the particular ease of someone settling in for a conversation they had been planning on the drive over.

"Did you look at the plan I sent?"

Theodore dipped the swab again. "I looked at it."

"And?"

"It's thorough."

Evan waited. Theodore continued working.

"Dad. It's the same plan I sent in the spring. And before that."

"I know."

"And you still haven't said anything about it."

Theodore wiped another thin strip of varnish from the painting. The blue deepened. "I've been busy."

Evan exhaled quietly, not quite a sigh. He had learned not to push too hard in the workshop. The shop had its own rhythm, and Theodore would not be hurried inside it.

After a moment, Evan said, "You know the brand project I told you about? The furniture company?"

"The one selling reproductions."

"Vintage-inspired reproductions," Evan said. "They've been talking about craftsmanship all week. Storytelling. Authenticity. They're building an entire marketing campaign around it." He gestured at the painting. "And you're standing here doing the real thing. Nobody knows."

Theodore shrugged slightly. "People buy what they want."

Evan studied him for a moment. Then he pulled out his phone and tapped the screen. "Just listen to this. Two minutes."

Theodore glanced up, mildly suspicious.

"I've been trying to get you to listen to this podcast for three months," Evan said. "Just this part. That's all I'm asking."

He turned the volume up and held the phone toward his father.

A woman's voice filled the quiet workshop.

"Most leaders don't struggle because they lack skill," the voice said. "They struggle because they question whether what they do still matters."

Theodore's hand paused above the painting.

Evan lowered the volume slightly. "Sound familiar?"

Theodore resumed his work. "You're projecting."

"Maybe," Evan said. "Or maybe you've spent thirty years doing work most people can't do, and nobody outside this room knows it exists."

Theodore set the cotton swab down and leaned back from the easel. The painting's sky now stretched across a brighter patch of blue than when he had started.

Evan studied the canvas. "That's incredible," he said quietly. The enthusiasm was gone from his voice. Stating the fact of it.

Theodore looked at the painting for a long moment.

He had always trusted that something valuable remained beneath the surface. The work was simply removing the layers hiding it.

He knew how to do that with art.

He wasn't sure he knew how to do it with a business.

Evan was still holding the phone.

"Just look at it," he said, holding the phone a little closer. "The mastermind thing. That's it."

Theodore wiped his hands on a cloth and took the phone. The screen showed a simple page describing a leadership mastermind for business owners navigating growth, change, and uncertainty.

He studied the description longer than he expected to. Across the workshop, his father's lamp held its steady circle of light over the workbench, the same as it always had.

Finally, he handed the phone back.

"Send me the link," he said.

Evan tried not to look surprised. "Already did."

Theodore turned back to the easel and picked up the cotton swab again. Sometimes restoration began with a simple decision, not to discard something, but to believe it was still worth uncovering.

He leaned closer to the canvas and carefully removed another thin layer of varnish. The color beneath deepened as the sky slowly returned to life.

Theodore named a number.

• • •

Miles away, a small torch flickered to life.

Jade Alvarez steadied her hands at her jeweler's bench as molten silver began to soften beneath the flame. Where Theodore spent his days revealing beauty hidden by time, Jade created pieces meant to be worn close to the heart.

Yet despite spending her days crafting symbols of love, Jade carried a quiet question she had never fully answered.

What if the one thing she didn't believe was that she herself was lovable?

CHAPTER 5

Jade Alvarez, Jade's Gems and Jewels

The small torch hissed softly as Jade Alvarez leaned over her jeweler's bench, adjusting the flame until it narrowed into a steady blue point. The silver band in the clamp had just begun to glow, the metal softening under the heat as she guided the solder carefully into the seam.

The join closed almost invisibly.

She set the torch aside and lifted the ring with tweezers, lowering it into the small bowl of water beside her bench. Steam curled upward for a moment before dissolving into the quiet of the shop.

At the front of the shop, she could hear Maya unlocking the display cases, the soft click of each latch familiar as a morning greeting.

Three of her four staff had keys. All of them had been with her at least two years. They knew the inventory, the systems, the way Jade liked the cases arranged by stone type rather than price point. What they did not have was Jade's presence with a customer. She had never fully figured out how to hand that part over.

Morning light poured through the tall front windows of Jade's Gems and Jewels, catching the edges of the glass display cases lining the walls. Inside them sat rows of necklaces, bracelets, and rings resting on dark velvet cushions. Each piece represented something different to the person who would eventually buy it. Engagements. Anniversaries. Birthdays. Reconciliations. Quiet promises people hoped would last longer than words sometimes did.

Jade dried the ring and turned it slowly between her fingers. The band was simple but balanced, the kind of piece that looked effortless even though it took hours to make it feel that way.

She set it on the velvet display pad and stepped back.

In the six years since she had opened Jade's Gems and Jewels, she had learned that people didn't come in for jewelry exactly. They came in for the moment the jewelry would mark. The couple who had driven two hours for an engagement ring because a friend said Jade would listen before she ever opened a case. The woman who had stood at the counter for forty minutes describing her mother before Jade picked up a single stone. The man who came back three times before he could say what he actually needed, and left with a piece that said it for him.

The display cases along the front wall caught the morning light, rows of necklaces, bracelets, and rings resting on dark velvet cushions. Each one waiting for the person who would give it meaning.

Jade had built something real here. She knew that on most days.

For a moment, she thought about another ring.

Her mother kept it in a small velvet box tucked in the back of her dresser drawer. Jade had found it once when she was eight, turning the diamond carefully in her palm while her mother folded laundry across the room.

"That used to be my wedding ring," her mother had said gently when she noticed Jade holding it.

"Why don't you wear it anymore?" Jade had asked.

Her mother had paused before answering. "Sometimes things change."

The ring went back into the box after that. Jade rarely saw it again.

The bell above the shop door chimed. Maya was closer to the door. Jade set the torch aside, pulled off her safety glasses, and walked to the front anyway. The couple stepped inside, their eyes moving immediately to the display cases. 'Hi,' Jade said with a warm smile. "What brings you in today?"

Behind her, Maya returned to the inventory she had been counting.

The woman laughed nervously. "We're looking for engagement rings."

Jade unlocked one of the cases and slid out a tray of designs, setting it gently on the glass counter. As the couple leaned closer, the stones caught the sunlight and scattered small flashes of light across the surface.

She began asking the questions she always asked. How they met. What kind of style felt like them. Whether they imagined something traditional or something more personal. Listening to their story was her favorite part of the process. People rarely came in just for aesthetics. They came in for meaning. They wanted a piece representing something permanent.

Eventually, the couple selected a design and promised to return the following week to finalize the order. When the door closed behind them, the shop settled again into its familiar quiet.

Jade returned to the bench and sat down, glancing at the two sketches at the top of her notebook.

New York Fashion Week.

Or the boutique collective showcase.

Fashion Week meant exposure. Press. Visibility. The kind of stage elevating a designer's reputation overnight if the right editors notice.

The boutique showcase was smaller and quieter. Independent shop owners gathered to select exclusive designers for their stores. Fewer cameras. Fewer headlines. But potentially deeper relationships.

She could only afford to do one. And she was not the only one it affected. Her team of four had been talking about Fashion Week since January. Maya had already started sketching display concepts. The decision Jade kept framing as a business strategy question was also a question about what she was willing to ask her people to build toward.

Her phone buzzed lightly against the wooden surface of the bench. A message from her brother.

Check this out. Thought of you.

Below it was an Instagram link.

She tapped it open.

The post showed a woman standing at the front of a small room filled with business owners seated around a long table. The caption read:

Leadership Mastermind for Creative Entrepreneurs – Applications Open

Jade frowned slightly. Leadership programs had never appealed to her. Most of them seemed designed for people who spoke comfortably about strategy, scaling, and market positioning. Jade spent her days sketching designs, selecting stones, and listening to customers tell her the stories their jewelry would represent.

She typed back.

I design jewelry. I'm not a leadership person.

His reply came fast.

You run a company, Jade. A real one. That counts.

Then, a few seconds later:

Just schedule a call. No commitment. What's the worst that happens?

She could think of several answers to that question. She kept them to herself.

Her eyes drifted back to the notebook.

Fashion Week meant stepping into a room where designers competed for attention. The boutique showcase meant working with people who had already decided they were looking for someone.

One path required being seen.

The other meant being chosen.

Jade knew which one felt safer.

She opened the link again. The page described a small mastermind group for founders navigating business decisions, growth, and leadership challenges. It started with a one-on-one conversation with the facilitator before the group met together.

A button sat at the bottom of the page.

Schedule an introductory session.

She tapped it before she had time to reconsider. The confirmation arrived within seconds.

Jade set the phone down and looked up.

Across the shop, the display cases caught the last of the afternoon light, each piece resting on dark velvet as though it had always belonged there.

• • •

Across the city, Emily Carter was preparing to meet the five business owners who had recently scheduled conversations with her.

Jade Alvarez would be one of them.

CHAPTER 6

Emily Carter, Executive Coach

She had done this enough times to know the first call was rarely about what it claimed to be.

People scheduled for a reason they could name. A business decision. A growth question. A team problem. Something concrete enough to justify the time. What they were actually carrying usually surfaced somewhere in the middle, sometimes in the last two minutes, occasionally not until the third session.

Emily had learned not to chase it.

She set a mug of tea on her desk, opened her laptop, and let the first call come to her.

Jade

Jade joined late, slightly breathless, a workbench visible behind her, scattered with stones and wire and the particular productive disorder of someone who had been working right up until the moment she stopped.

"Sorry. A customer stayed longer than I expected."

"Take a breath," Emily said.

Jade laughed, surprised. She breathed. "Okay. Hi."

"Hi. What's behind you?"

Jade glanced back. "Everything, basically. I design here, build here, meet clients here." She turned back to the screen. "It might not be huge, but it's mine."

"What does it feel like when you're in there working?"

"Safe." No hesitation. "Like I know exactly what I'm doing."

"And right now? On this call?"

Jade smiled. "Less sure."

She recovered quickly, leaning forward slightly. "Can I ask you something first? About how the group works."

"Of course."

"How many people? And what industries? Because I'm not sure I'm the right fit for something designed for, I don't know, corporate executives or whatever."

Emily described the group. Jade listened, nodded, asked a follow-up about the individual sessions, then another about confidentiality, then one about scheduling. Each question was genuine. Each one also kept her on the asking side.

"You're good at questions," Emily said.

Jade laughed. "Occupational hazard. I spend all day asking customers what they actually want."

"What do you actually want?"

Jade opened her mouth and then closed it.

"From the group," Emily added. "What would make this worth your time?"

"Honestly?" Jade looked at her hands. She turned a thin bracelet once around her wrist. "I have a decision I've been putting off for weeks. Two opportunities. I can only do one. And every time I sit down to think it through, I end up just..." She paused. "Rearranging the variables."

"Tell me about them."

Jade described Fashion Week and the boutique showcase with the fluency of someone who had turned the options over many times. The exposure versus the relationship. The visibility versus being chosen. The risk of the larger room.

"Which one pulls at you?" Emily asked.

"Fashion Week." Quickly. Then: "But it terrifies me."

"What's the terror?"

Jade was quiet in a way she hadn't been quiet for the whole call. Not thinking. Something else.

"Walking into a room where no one has decided they want you yet," she said finally.

Emily didn't say anything.

"And the boutique show feels safer because someone already rang the bell before you walk in," Jade continued, as if finishing a thought she'd started before the call. "Which I know is probably the whole problem."

"Is it a problem?"

Jade looked at her. "Isn't it?"

"I don't know yet," Emily said. "That's what we'd find out." She paused. "What I notice is you figured that out just now. In about thirty seconds. After weeks of rearranging variables."

Jade was still for a moment.

"The variables were easier," she said quietly.

"They usually are."

They talked through the logistics of the program. Jade asked two more questions, practical ones this time, and Emily answered them plainly. There was a pause at the end where the call could have gone either way.

"I'll think about it," Jade said. "The group, I mean."

"Of course."

"I'll think about it," she said again. Emily recognized when someone had already decided, but needed a moment to catch up to themselves.

Jade scheduled before they hung up.

Roman

Roman joined two minutes early. He had a notepad. He had done research.

"I want to be upfront," he said. "I'm not sure this is the right format for what I'm dealing with. The challenges I'm facing are operational. I appreciate your time, but I want to be clear about that going in."

"I appreciate the clarity," Emily said. "Tell me about them."

He did. It was organized and thorough — the kind of assessment he would present to a client, and she could tell he had prepared it well in advance. Acquisition opportunity. Boutique firm. Founder ready to retire, no successor. Financial projections reviewed twice. Integration risks mapped. Cultural overlap considered.

When he finished, Emily said, "Is there information you're still missing?"

"No. The data is largely there."

"So what's actually in the way?"

He looked toward the window. Something in his posture shifted, barely perceptible. "I want to make sure the analysis is complete before I bring a recommendation."

"You said the data is largely there."

"Largely."

"What's the missing piece?"

Roman was quiet for a moment. "I'm not sure I'd call it a missing piece exactly."

Emily waited.

"It's more that I want to be certain before I move."

"Certain of what?"

He picked up his pen. "That the decision is sound."

"You've reviewed the projections twice," Emily said. "You've mapped the risks. You've considered the cultural overlap. At what point would you have enough to feel certain?"

The question sat in the room.

Roman set the pen down. "I'm not sure I know the answer to that."

"That's interesting," Emily said. Not as a judgment. Just as an observation.

He looked at her. "Why?"

"Because you clearly know how to make decisions. You've been running a firm of forty-two people for three years. You've made hundreds of decisions in that time." She paused. "So the question isn't really whether you know how. It's what's different about this one."

Roman was quiet for longer than he had been quiet for anything in the call so far.

"My father would have decided by now," he said.

Emily let that sit.

"What does that mean to you?" she asked.

He picked up the pen again. Set it down. Looked toward the window. "I'm not sure this is what I came here to talk about."

"I know," Emily said.

He was quiet again. Outside the window, the city held its clean geometry, indifferent.

"He died three years ago," Roman said finally. "Without warning. No transition plan. The firm was suddenly mine, and the team was looking at me the following Monday." He paused. "I stabilized it. I did what needed to be done."

"Yes," Emily said.

"But this decision is different. This isn't maintaining what he built." He stopped. "This is deciding what comes next."

"And you've never done that before."

"No."

Emily looked at him. "What would it mean if you got it wrong?"

Roman's jaw tightened slightly. "The firm would be exposed. People would be affected."

"What would it mean about you?"

He was still for a long time.

"That I was only steady because I inherited something solid," he said. He said it the way someone reads a measurement off a gauge they've been avoiding looking at.

Emily didn't move to fill the silence.

After a moment, Roman said, "I don't think I've said that out loud before."

"No," Emily said. "It doesn't sound like something you'd say out loud."

He looked at her with the careful attention of someone recalibrating. "The people in this group. They're business owners?"

"Yes. Different industries, different pressures."

"And they work through things like this."

"They work through what's underneath things like this," Emily said. "Which turns out to be more useful."

Roman nodded slowly. He picked up his pen one more time, and this time he wrote something on the notepad.

"Send me the details," he said.

Cameron

Cameron joined from a truck cab, the window behind her showing a flat gray sky above a tree line. She had exactly thirty minutes. She made that clear before Emily had finished her greeting.

"The farm is working," she said. "Regenerative transition is on track. Soil health is improving, yields are coming back, supplier relationships are stable." She set her jaw slightly. "What isn't working is everything that happens when I stop doing and start deciding."

"Say more about that."

"Delegation. Long-term strategy. Trusting other people to handle things I could just handle myself." She said it the way someone recites a list of known problems. "I micromanage. I know I micromanage. I can see myself doing it, and I do it anyway."

"Why?"

"Because when something goes wrong, it's on me."

"It's on you either way," Emily said. "Whether you delegated it or did it yourself."

Cameron looked at her.

"So it's not really about the outcome," Emily said.

A pause. "What's it about then?"

"You tell me."

Cameron's eyes moved to the field beyond the window for a moment. A farmhand crossed the far edge, barely visible. She watched him for a second before looking back.

"My dad built this place," she said. "He's still around, still has opinions about how it should run. My sisters aren't involved. The older farmers in the county think regenerative is nonsense." She stopped. "I don't fit neatly anywhere."

"Not with the old guard," Emily said. "Not with your sisters."

"Not anywhere," Cameron said. It came out flatter and more honest than she intended.

Emily let it stand.

"When something goes wrong on the farm," she said, "what does the voice in your head say?"

Cameron's answer was immediate. "That I was never supposed to be the one running it."

Silence.

"You've built something real," Emily said. "The soil is coming back. You said that yourself in the first two minutes."

Cameron waited.

"So what are you still trying to prove?"

Cameron's expression shifted. Not agreement. Recognition.

"Is there a difference?" she said. "Practically speaking."

"You're asking me if this is practical," Emily asked.

"I run a farm. Everything has to be practical."

"Then practically speaking," Emily said, "the most expensive thing on your operation right now isn't a supplier contract or a distribution problem. It's the energy it costs you to keep proving something to yourself every single day."

Cameron was quiet for the first time in the call.

"Okay," she said finally. The word landed the way her words always landed. Like a decision made, filed, and already being acted on.

"Okay," Emily said.

Theodore

Theodore joined from his workshop. Frames and covered canvases lined the shelves behind him. His father's lamp threw a warm circle of light over his shoulder. He settled into his chair without hurrying, the way a man does when he has learned that stillness is its own form of precision.

"My son told me to call you," he said.

"What did you tell him?"

"That I'd think about it." The corner of his mouth moved slightly. "Three months ago."

"What changed?"

Theodore looked at something off-screen for a moment. "He played me something. A few seconds of a podcast." He paused. "It was about whether what you do still matters."

"Does it?" Emily asked. "Your work."

"To me." Without hesitation. "I'm less certain about anyone else."

"Tell me about the work."

He described it the way someone describes a room they've lived in their whole life. Without looking at it. Without realizing they love it. Restoration. Antiques. Paintings. The patience required to remove a century of varnish without disturbing what's underneath. The moment when the original color comes back.

Emily listened without interrupting.

When he finished, she said, "What's the shop called?"

"Sinclair Restorations. My father and uncle started it."

"And you took it over."

"When they were ready to step back, yes." He paused. "My father kept coming in for years after he retired. Whenever something interesting arrived." His thumb moved to the edge of his watchband. "Those were good years."

"When did he stop coming in?"

"Three years ago." Quietly. "He passed."

They sat with that for a moment.

"And since then," Emily said carefully, "you've been in the shop alone."

"Yes."

"Doing the same work."

"Yes."

"But it feels different."

Theodore looked at her. "How did you know that?"

"Because you said it feels like fading," Emily said. "Not failure. Fading. That's not a market problem. That's what happens when someone who understood the value of what you do is no longer there to confirm it."

Theodore was very still.

"Your son sees it," Emily said. "He keeps coming back with the same plan. He's trying to tell you something."

"He's trying to modernize the business."

"Is that what you think he's doing?"

Theodore didn't answer right away. His thumb moved along the watchband again, back and forth.

"He thinks the work deserves more visibility," he said finally.

"And you hear that as..."

"That it needs help." He stopped. "That what it is, isn't enough on its own."

"Is that what he said?"

Theodore looked toward the lamp for a long moment. "No," he said. "That's not what he said."

Emily let the quiet hold.

"Do people actually change?" Theodore asked eventually. "Or do they just understand things better?"

"Both," Emily said. "Understanding shifts something. Then the body catches up to the understanding."

He nodded once, slowly, filing it away.

"The program," he said. "Tell me how it works."

She did. He listened without interrupting, which she had come to understand was his form of full attention. At the end, he sat quietly for a moment.

"Send me the link," he said. "My son already did. But send it anyway."

Julia

Julia was already on the call when Emily connected, sitting in her bakery with a mug in both hands and the slightly too-bright energy of someone who had prepared to make a good impression.

"Hi. Sorry, I'm still at the shop. I hope that's okay."

"Of course," Emily said. "What time did you start this morning?"

"Four-thirty." Julia laughed softly. "Same as every day."

"Tell me what brought you here."

Julia set the mug down and sat up slightly. "Seven years," she said. "I've kept this place going for seven years. Built the regulars, built the reputation, outlasted most of the competition." A brief smile. "I love it. I genuinely love it. But lately I wake up early, and I can't remember why it used to feel like enough."

"What did it used to feel like?"

Something crossed her face and was gone before she could decide what to do with it.

"Like I was building something," she said. Then faster: "I still am. It's a good bakery. Really good. I just need to figure out the next step, and I think I've been overthinking it, honestly, because the bones are good and the regulars are loyal and I just need a clearer strategy, probably, or maybe—"

"Julia."

She stopped.

"You said it used to feel like enough," Emily said. "Past tense."

Julia looked at her mug.

"What changed?"

"The industry changed," Julia said. "New competitors, social media, younger demographics who want a whole aesthetic experience, not just good bread." She nodded slightly, settling into the explanation. "It's a different landscape than it was seven years ago."

"That's true," Emily said. "When did it start feeling different to you personally?"

Julia was quiet.

"The industry has been changing for longer than a year," Emily said. "You said you've been keeping up, mostly. So the landscape isn't new." She paused. "What's new?"

Julia glanced toward the back of the shop. At the open office door, at something inside it, then back at the screen.

"A lot changed about a year ago," she said.

"Tell me about that."

A pause. The brightness in Julia's face was still there, but it had shifted, become something she was holding rather than something that came naturally.

"I had someone," she said carefully. "We were building this together. He had the business mind, I had the kitchen. It worked." She stopped. "He got an opportunity, and he took it. I stayed." She shrugged, easy and practiced. "It was the right call. For both of us."

"And since then?"

"Since then, I've been running it alone." Another practiced shrug. "Which is fine. I'm fine. I just think I need someone in my corner who understands the business side, which is probably why I'm here actually, because the creative part I can do, it's really the strategy—"

"You're doing it again," Emily said gently.

Julia looked at her.

"The pivot," Emily said. "Back to strategy. Back to what's practical." She held Julia's gaze. "What does it feel like in your body right now, when you think about the bakery?"

Julia was quiet for a long moment.

"Hollow," she said. She seemed surprised by the word.

"Yes," Emily said.

Neither of them spoke for a moment.

"The strategy questions are real," Emily said. "We'll get to them. But underneath the strategy there's something else and I think you already know what it is." She paused. "You've been running on a particular kind of fuel for a year. The fuel of proving you didn't need to go. And that fuel works, until it doesn't."

Julia looked at her mug. When she looked up, her eyes were steady but different from what they had been at the start of the call.

"I'll think about the group," she said.

"Of course."

"I just want to make sure it's the right fit," she said. "I'll think about it and let you know."

"Take your time," Emily said.

When the last call ended, Emily closed the laptop and sat quietly for a moment.

Five different people. Five different businesses.

One city.

She picked up her mug, found it had gone cold, and set it back down.

She opened her notebook and wrote a single line at the bottom of the page.

They're ready.

• • •

The building was on a side street she hadn't been to before. Cameron found a parking spot on the first pass, which felt like the wrong kind of luck.

She turned off the engine.

Through the windshield, she could see the entrance. A woman she didn't recognize went in. Then a man in a jacket. She didn't know either of them, and that was fine. That was the point, probably.

She had the address written on a piece of paper folded in the breast pocket of her jacket. She had it memorized. She'd written it down anyway.

She thought about the drive back. Thirty minutes if traffic was reasonable. She could be home before noon. There was a section of the south pasture that needed walking. There was always something that needed walking.

She put her hand on the key.

She didn't turn it.

She sat there longer than she needed to. A pigeon landed on the sidewalk in front of the truck, picked at something, and flew away. A woman came out of the building, not the same woman who had gone in. She was on her phone, laughing at something, and she didn't look at the truck or the person in it.

Cameron thought about her father. Not anything specific he'd said. Just the shape of him at the kitchen table that morning when she'd told him where she was going. He had looked at his coffee.

She opened the door and got out.

She didn't look at the paper.

Part 2

CHAPTER 7

The First Circle

Emily preferred to arrive early enough to let the room settle around her before anyone else walked in.

She poured a glass of water, set her folder at the head of the table, and sat. The room was a standard conference room: oval table, eight chairs, recessed lighting slightly too bright. Someone had angled the blinds against the afternoon sun, leaving the room cut diagonally, half lit and half in shade. She left them as they were.

Jade was the first to arrive, and she came in already smiling. "I'm so glad to meet you in person finally," she said, extending her hand to Emily before she'd even set her bag down. "I've been telling everyone about this. My best friend, my two closest clients --" She laughed briefly. "Sorry. I'm a lot at first."

She wasn't, particularly. But she moved toward the window chair and started arranging things in front of her with the focused, quiet energy of someone who settled through their hands. A sketchbook. A bracelet she slid from her wrist and set beside it. A pen she uncapped and recapped twice.

Roman came in next, two minutes before the hour. He paused briefly at the threshold, took in the room, chose a seat two chairs from the head of the table on the left side, set a leather planner down, and did not open it. He poured himself some water and gave Emily a small nod.

"Roman," she said.

"Emily."

Cameron arrived in a navy athletic jacket with last season's Ag Expo logo faded at the cuff. One pass of the room and she had it. She sat directly across from Jade, set a coffee cup down, put a pencil at the top of a blank page, and was ready. She had the quality of someone with hours already behind her and no particular interest in counting what was left.

Theodore came through the door the way he moved through everything. Without hurry. He stood for a moment just inside the room, as though letting it register him rather than the other way around. Then he crossed to a chair near the end of the table, straightened his cuffs before he sat, and folded his hands. A gold watch caught the overhead light. His thumb moved once to its edge, then stilled.

Julia was last, slightly flushed, a strand of hair loose from a bun that had been precise earlier in the day. She had flour in the seams of her jeans. She looked around the table with a smile that tried to reach everyone at once and said, "Hi. I own a bakery a few blocks from here. You should all come by."

A few people smiled back.

Emily looked around the table once. Five people who had each said yes to something they weren't entirely sure about. She had heard it in every call. The pause before the yes. The thing it cost them to show up.

"Thank you for being here," she said. "It takes something to walk into a room like this. I don't take that lightly." She looked around the table, unhurried. "I'd like us to take a few minutes to introduce ourselves. I'll start."

She settled back in her chair.

"I'm Emily Carter. I'm an executive coach. I have two books and a podcast, which some of you have probably found." A small smile, general, not directed. "I work with people who have already built something real and are wondering why getting to the next level feels like it would cost more than they have left to give."

She paused.

"I grew up watching my parents build a construction company together from nothing. My dad had strong opinions about how it should run. My mom was half-owner, but her voice didn't always carry equal weight, and after a while, she stopped trying to make it." She said it plainly, no bitterness in it. "Eventually, they divorced. My dad took over the business. And I watched something that worked become something that didn't. Not because the work was wrong. Because of what nobody ever said out loud. The divorce just made it visible."

She looked around the table.

"That's what I do now. Most leaders don't know what's running in the background. They just feel they're giving everything, yet something still limits them. I help them find it, name it, and decide whether it still belongs there."

A pause.

"Who's next?"

Jade leaned forward slightly, like she'd been waiting for the opening. "I'll start." She glanced around the table with the ease of someone who had learned early how to make a room comfortable. "I'm Jade. I design jewelry, mostly custom pieces for people marking something. Engagements, anniversaries, the kind of moments people want to hold onto." She turned her pen once in her fingers. "I have a boutique. Small but mine, and I love it." A brief pause. "I also have a decision I've been avoiding for about six weeks, which is probably why I'm here."

She said it lightly, but it landed.

Cameron set her coffee cup down. "I'll go." No transition, no warm-up. "Cameron Miller. Miller's Harvest. We farm about four hundred acres, which has been in my family four generations. I run a crew of thirty to forty full-time, more during planting and harvest. I'm transitioning to regenerative organic, which means I'm fighting the soil, the margins, the co-op buyers, my crew's resistance, and my father more or less simultaneously."

She picked up her pencil.

"I'm here because something's got to give, and I'm afraid it's going to be me." She seemed mildly surprised she'd said it out loud. "That's it."

The room was quiet for a moment.

Theodore waited until the quiet had finished settling before he spoke.

"Theodore Sinclair. My father started a restoration shop about fifty years ago. Antique furniture, paintings, pieces people thought were too far gone." His thumb moved to the edge of his watch without him seeming to notice. "My father passed three years ago. I've been running it alone since." He paused. "My son has been trying to get me to modernize for at least a year. I keep telling him I'll think about it." The corner of his mouth moved slightly. "I'm still thinking about it."

Roman looked at the table for a moment, then spoke.

"Roman Hale. Hale and Co. Architects. My father founded it. My father also passed three years ago. I took over when he died without a transition plan." He set his hands flat on the planner in front of him. "The firm is stable. More profitable than when I inherited it." A small pause. "There's an acquisition on the table. Boutique firm, strong reputation, founder ready to retire. The data is largely there, but..."

He stopped. His jaw tightened slightly, just once.

He didn't finish the sentence.

Julia tucked the loose strand back into her bun, which didn't hold, and smiled at the room. "I'm Julia. I own The French Bakery, two locations now, the original about three blocks from here. I bought it seven years ago from the original owner and kept the name." She laughed softly as she noticed flour smeared on her jeans. "I've been baking since four-thirty this morning, in case anyone was wondering."

She looked up. For just a second, something real moved under the warmth. Then she smiled at the room.

"You all should come by," she said. "Seriously. I'll send you home with something."

Emily looked around the table. Each of them had given the room a version of themselves. Some had given more than they planned to. She had heard it in the sentences that stopped short, the things offered almost accidentally.

"Before we go further, I want to tell you how this works." Her voice was unhurried. "We meet as a group six times, about every other week. In between, each of you also gets six individual sessions with me, approximately every other week. The group work is shared. The individual work is yours. What you bring from one into the other is always your choice."

"Now." She looked at the table. "Let's do something you probably haven't done since you got up this morning. Find a comfortable position. Close your eyes if that works for you. We're going to check in with your body before we do anything else."

Chairs shifted. A notebook is closed. The hallway noise faded into the background.

"We're going to start with your feet. Just notice where your feet touch the floor. The pressure. The angle. Are they flat? Tucked back? Resting lightly?"

Roman cleared his throat. "Is this standard practice in executive coaching?"

Emily smiled. "Only when strategy isn't the real problem."

She continued. "Notice your toes. Go ahead and try to wiggle them. Notice you can't really move just one at a time, especially that middle one. They kind of have to go together."

Julia pressed her shoes flat against the carpet. Jade experimented with one toe at a time, the faintest smile touching her lips when they stubbornly moved together. Cameron opened one eye, then closed it again. Roman didn't move at first. Then, reluctantly, his shoe shifted.

Theodore's eyes were already closed. He had been ready before she started.

"Your feet carry you all day. We rarely pay attention to them. Just observe."

Emily's voice stayed steady.

"Now notice your ankles. The angle they're at. Move up to your calves. Are they tight? Relaxed? Sore? There's no right answer. We're just observing."

The room grew quieter.

"Scan up to your knees. Notice the bend. Then your thighs. Notice which part of your legs is touching the chair. The fabric. The support."

The tension broke. Someone shifted deeper into their seat.

"Bring awareness to your hips and your lower back. We hold a lot here without realizing it. Is there tension? Or ease?"

Another pause.

"Now your stomach. Your chest. Notice your breath. Notice the rise. The fall."

Someone exhaled. Then someone else.

"Let's move up your spine. Now to your shoulders. This is often where we carry our stress. We even say 'the weight of the world is on your shoulders'. Just notice. No fixing."

Roman's jaw loosened. Theodore's posture softened by degrees.

"Now your neck. The place where your neck meets your skull. We don't pay much attention to that space. Just scan it. Notice."

Her voice lowered slightly.

"Your jaw. Is it clenched? Resting? Let it hang open just enough to check."

Jade swallowed and relaxed her mouth. Cameron rolled her shoulders once, then stilled.

"Your forehead. Your temples. The top of your head. If there's tension, simply notice it. If there isn't, notice that too."

She let the quiet stretch a moment.

"Okay." Her voice was calm and intentional. "Bring your attention back to your neck and shoulders."

A few people subtly shifted. Someone swallowed.

"We carry a lot there," Emily continued. "Even the people who swear they don't."

Cameron's mouth twitched as if she might disagree. She didn't.

Emily looked around the table. "Would anyone be willing to walk through this next part out loud? Everyone else can do it silently. No pressure. But it's different when we can hear an example."

Jade's bracelets clinked as she lifted her hand halfway, like she was asking permission from herself.

"I'll try," she said. "If that's okay."

Emily nodded once. "Perfect. Close your eyes if that feels okay. And don't perform this. Just share what comes."

Jade let out a small breath. "Okay."

"Check in," Emily said. "Notice your shoulders right now."

Jade's shoulders rose the tiniest bit. "They're tight. Like they're trying to live inside my ears."

A couple of people smiled quietly, recognizing themselves in the sentence.

"Good. Don't try to relax it. We're just going to observe it."

Emily waited.

"I want you to find the edges of that tension. Just kind of scan around it. Does it go up into your neck? Does it spread out toward your shoulders? Take your time. Just notice where it starts and where it stops."

Jade was quiet for a moment. "It starts at my shoulders. Bunches up at the neck."

"Okay. So it's got some size to it." Emily didn't rush. "When you draw a line around the whole thing, does it have a shape? Sometimes it's round. Sometimes it's more of a rectangle. Some people see a hanger shape because it goes up the neck and out across the shoulders. What does it look like to you?"

Jade's brow pulled in slightly. "Long. Oval. Thicker in the middle."

"Good. Long oval, thicker in the middle." She said it back like it mattered. "Now notice if it's moving in any way. Is it pulling? Pushing? Twisting? What is that tension actually doing?"

"Pulling up. Like it's trying to hold something."

"Okay." She let that land. "Sometimes tension has a temperature. Hot, cold, or just the same as the rest of your body. What do you notice?"

"Warm. Not hot."

"Warm. Good." The smallest shift in her voice. "Sometimes when people really zoom in, they notice a color. Not everyone does, and that's fine. Do you sense a color?"

"Orange."

"Warm orange oval, pulling upward." Emily let that sit for a second. "Last thing. What's the texture when you really settle in close to it? Smooth like glass? Rough like an orange peel? Rocky? Dense?"

"Dense." Jade closed her eyes again. "Like clay."

"Good. Now just notice it. Nothing to change. Nothing to solve."

She gave Jade a moment.

"I want you to observe it the way you'd look at a sculpture in a museum. Walk all the way around it in your mind. See what it looks like from above, from the side. When you really settle in close, does anything shift?"

"It gets a little smaller when I focus on it."

"That happens." Emily didn't make it a big deal. "Now I want you to relax into it. Not push it away. Not try to release it. Just ease into it the way you'd slide into a hot tub. It's not hurting you. It's just a sensation. There's just a warm orange clay oval sitting in your neck. That's it."

Jade's shoulders dropped slightly.

"When you relax into it like that, does it get bigger, smaller, or stay the same?"

"Less intense."

"Good." Emily waited. "Now this next part might feel a little strange." She said it matter-of-factly, like someone warning you about a speed bump. "I want you to send it some gratitude. It's there because it has something for you. It is not the enemy. So whatever that looks like for you, just send it some thanks."

Jade's brow pulled in slightly. But she did it.

The room stayed quiet.

"Does anything change when you do that?"

"It's lighter."

"Good. Now we're going to hand it a microphone." Emily let that land before continuing. "Think of one of those little karaoke mics. You're going to hold it out and ask, What have you got for me? Then just notice what comes. It might be a word. It might be an image. A memory might surface. Don't edit it. Don't decide if it makes sense. Just notice what floats through."

Jade was quiet for a moment. "I don't have to keep score."

She didn't sound certain it was right.

Emily didn't fill the silence. Then: "What does that mean to you?"

Jade opened her eyes partway. "I don't know. That's just what came."

"Okay. Sit with it. When you really let it land, what happens to the clay?"

Jade closed her eyes again. Something moved across her face. "It's softer."

Emily waited. "Is there someone you've been keeping score with?"

Longer silence.

"My dad."

Emily didn't react. "Take a breath. Notice your shoulders."

Jade inhaled slowly. "It's fading."

Emily let that sit. The room had gone very still. Roman had stopped moving entirely.

She looked around the table. "Everyone, check in with your own shoulders. Just notice what shifted, if anything. If nothing shifted, that's fine. The goal isn't instant relief. The goal is awareness."

She paused, her voice turning a shade more direct.

"Your nervous system doesn't belong in fight, flight, or freeze while you're trying to lead people. If your body is carrying something, it will show up. In your tone. Your patience. Your decisions. Your relationships. Your sleep."

Cameron exhaled hard through her nose.

Roman's jaw tightened. Subtle. Automatic.

Emily looked back at Jade. "Thank you for going first."

Jade's smile was small but real. "I didn't think that was going to work."

"Most people don't," Emily said, without fanfare, and moved.

She gathered a small stack of papers from her folder and slid them down the table, one to each person.

"Before you look at it, I want to tell you what this isn't." She settled back in her chair. "It's not a test. There's no grade. I'll see your numbers, and I'll use them to understand where you are. That's it."

She looked around the table.

"Everyone who does this gets surprised by something. Including people who were pretty sure they wouldn't."

She let them pick up the papers.

"Think of somewhere you feel challenged right now. Something you're trying to grow into, or a decision that's been sitting heavy. Whatever came to mind when you signed up for this is probably it. Don't overthink it. Just hold that area."

She paused while the room settled.

"I'm going to read seven statements. For each one, rate how true it feels right now, in that area. Scale of one to ten. Ten means completely true. One means it doesn't feel true at all."

She looked up. "Don't analyze it. Don't justify it. Just write the first number that comes to mind. Your thinking brain will want to explain the number. Let it wait."

Chairs shifted. Someone uncapped a pen. Theodore straightened the paper in front of him with one careful motion.

"First statement," Emily said. "In this area where you feel challenged: on a scale of one to ten, how true is it that I am enough?"

The room went quiet in a way it hadn't before. Not uncomfortable exactly. Just honest.

Jade's pen hovered for a moment before she wrote. Julia looked at the paper a bit longer than necessary. Cameron wrote quickly, then set her pen down like she didn't want to look at the number.

Roman held his pen without moving it. Then he wrote.

"Don't overthink," Emily said. "Or judge, just write."

She waited until the pens went still.

"In this area where you feel challenged: on a scale of one to ten, how true is it that I am worthy?"

Theodore shifted in his chair. His thumb moved to the edge of his watch without him seeming to notice.

Emily read the rest at the same steady pace. No inflection. No editorializing.

I am valuable.

I am lovable.

A small sound from Roman. Not quite a laugh. Not quite a scoff. Somewhere between the two.

Emily glanced at him without stopping. "Go ahead and give it a number anyway," she said, easily. "Even if the word feels strange. Especially then."

He looked back at the paper.

I trust myself.

I have what it takes.

I belong.

The last one landed differently in the room. Something about the plainness of it. Several people wrote slowly.

Emily let the silence run for a moment after the last statement.

"Now I want you to do it one more time," she said. "But this time, think of somewhere you feel genuinely confident. Something you're good at, something that comes naturally."

The energy in the room shifted. Shoulders lifted slightly. Julia brightened. Cameron's jaw unclenched.

"Same seven statements. Same scale."

She read them again. This time, the pens moved faster.

When the last one was done, Emily set her own page down.

"Go ahead and look at the two sets of numbers side by side."

Quiet.

"Most of you are going to see a gap," she said. "A real one. Between the area where you feel challenged and the area where you feel confident." She paused. "That gap isn't about intelligence. It isn't about effort. It isn't about how hard you've worked or how capable you actually are."

"It's a story running in the background. One you wrote a long time ago, when you were young enough that it made sense to write it that way. Your brain did exactly what it was supposed to do. It made meaning out of something that happened. And then it filed that meaning away and never revisited it."

She looked around the table.

"Some of us are running on interpretations we formed when we were eight years old or younger. Not because we're broken. Because we don't realize it, and nobody told us we could go back and update them."

"We're going to spend our time together learning to see those stories clearly. Not to beat ourselves up about them. Just to understand where they came from." She looked around the table, unhurried. "That's where things start to shift."

Emily let them sit with the papers for a moment before she spoke.

"Your scores are yours. You don't have to share them with the group. Not today, not ever, unless you choose to." She paused. "I'm going to collect these at the end of today and get them back to you before your first individual session. That's where we'll look at them together and talk about what they mean for you specifically."

A few shoulders eased.

"But if anything came up while you were filling this out, something surprising or landed harder than you expected, I'd love to hear it. No obligation. Just if you want to."

Jade spoke first, turning her bracelet over in her fingers. "I scored lower than I thought I would on a few of these. Especially the one about having what it takes." She shrugged. "Seeing it as a number is different than just feeling it."

"Of course it is," Emily said.

Cameron set her paper face down. "I know what my challenges are. I didn't need a form to tell me." A short breath. "But the belonging one." She stopped. "That one I didn't expect."

Emily nodded once. "Sometimes those are the ones worth paying attention to."

Roman rubbed the back of his neck. "Some of these felt irrelevant to why I'm here." He glanced at the paper. "But I noticed I had to think longer on a few of them than I expected to."

"That's useful information," Emily said.

Julia looked at the table for a moment. "I scored lower than I expected on a few of them." She glanced toward the back of the room briefly, at nothing visible, then back. "The business ones especially." She smiled, easy and practiced. "Which probably just means I need a better strategy."

She said it like she believed it. Almost.

Theodore cleared his throat. He didn't look up. "The self-trust one. It's one I recognize."

"That's enough to start," Emily said.

She stood and walked around the table as she collected the papers.

"What you just did takes more courage than most people realize. You showed up, you did a body scan, and you put honest numbers on things that are easier to leave vague." She tucked the papers into her folder.

"One thing before you go. This week, a few times a day, check in with your shoulders. That's it. Not when something big happens. Just randomly. Driving to work, sitting in a meeting, making dinner. Notice what's there."

She looked around the table.

"You don't have to do anything with it. Just start getting curious about what your body's been doing while you weren't paying attention."

A few nods around the table.

Emily caught Julia's eye as people began to gather their things. "Let's get your first individual session on the calendar before you go."

One by one, they gathered their things. Roman was the last to leave. He paused at the door, hand on the frame, like he was going to say something. Then he didn't.

CHAPTER 8

Julia, What It Actually Takes

Emily was already on the call when Julia connected, which Julia hadn't expected. She had been bracing for the awkward wait of a blank screen.

"Hi," Julia said, slightly flushed. She was still in the bakery. The display cases were dark behind her, the kitchen quiet in the particular way it only got after closing. "Sorry, I almost rescheduled."

"I'm glad you didn't," Emily said. "How are you?"

"Good. Fine." Julia laughed softly. "Tired. But that's just Tuesday."

"How was the morning?"

"Four-thirty." Julia reached for the mug beside her. "Same as every day. We sold out of the lavender shortbread by nine, which is either a good sign or a sign I need to make more."

"Which do you think it is?"

Julia paused, slightly surprised by the question. "Both, probably."

Emily smiled. "Before we get into the work, I want to check in on last week. The group session. How did it go for you?"

Julia set the mug down and looked at it for a moment. "Honestly? Better than I expected." She glanced up. "I thought I'd feel more exposed. But everyone was just…" She paused. "In it. You know?"

"I noticed that too."

"Jade going first helped." Julia smiled. "I don't think she knows how much."

"She might," Emily said. "Okay. So today, we're going to look at your assessment results and then work on whichever belief makes the most sense to start with. Does that feel okay?"

"Yes." Julia nodded. "I've been thinking about it, actually. The numbers."

"Good. That's exactly the right thing to be thinking about." Emily opened her folder. "Let me show you what I see."

She walked Julia through the two sets of numbers side by side. Julia had scored herself on expanding the bakery in a competitive market for the growth domain. For the confidence domain, she had chosen her relationship with customers, connecting one-on-one, as part of the work she trusted completely.

The gap was visible immediately.

"So the customer connection side," Emily said. "Eights and nines across the board. I trust myself, I have what it takes, I am enough. Those are real numbers."

Julia nodded. "That part doesn't scare me."

"And the expansion side." Emily paused on the screen. "The one that caught my eye is here. I have what it takes. You scored yourself a three."

Julia looked at the number. "Yeah."

"Not a four. Not a five. A three."

"I know." She said it quietly.

"What does three feel like when you say it out loud?"

Julia was quiet for a moment. "Like I already knew it was true and didn't want to admit it."

Emily let that sit.

"The other one I want to name," Emily said, "is I trust myself. You scored a four on the expansion side and a nine on the customer side. That's a five-point gap." She paused. "Same person. Same week. Five points apart depending on the context."

Julia looked at the numbers. "I hadn't noticed that one."

"That's often how it works. The belief we're most aware of isn't always the one doing the most work." Emily closed the folder slightly. "So here's what I want to suggest. We start with I have what it takes today. Not because the others don't matter. Because this one is loudest right now."

Julia nodded slowly.

"Does that feel right in your body when I say it?"

Julia almost deflected. She caught herself. "Yes," she said. "It does."

"It might be," Emily said. "We'll find out. That's exactly where we're going."

"I want to give you a scenario. Stay with me."

Emily leaned slightly toward the camera.

"Your landlord calls you tomorrow morning. The space next door has been a dry cleaner for eleven years. They're closing at the end of the year. He's offering you first right of refusal. You could double your footprint. New equipment, real catering capacity, room to grow the team. But it means a five-year lease and real debt."

She waited.

"Now sit in that. The opportunity is real. The call just happened. And the thought comes up: I don't have what it takes. When you think that thought, notice what happens in your body. Not your thoughts about it. Your body."

Julia went quiet.

"There it is," Emily said. "Tell me where you feel it."

"It's like a dropping sensation. Right in the middle."

"Good. I want you to stay with it. Don't try to explain it or talk yourself out of it. Just notice it."

Julia closed her eyes.

"Can you find the edges of it? Scan from the outside in. Where does it start and where does it stop?"

Quiet.

"It's not my whole stomach," Julia said. "More concentrated. Like a circle. Maybe the size of a fist."

"Okay, fist-sized, round." Emily moved without making it complicated. "Is there a temperature to it? Hot, cold, or just body temperature?"

"Cold. Definitely cold."

"Is there a color that comes?"

Julia was quiet for a moment. "Black. Or very dark gray."

"Is there a texture?"

"Heavy. Like wet sand."

Emily let her stay with it.

"So we have a cold, dark grey, fist-sized circle in your stomach. Just observe it. We're not trying to get rid of it. We're not trying to fix it. It's just there."

A pause.

"Let's zoom in on it. Like you're at an art museum, and this is an exhibit you've never seen before."

Another pause.

"When you zoom in and study it, does it change in any way?"

Julia scrunches her nose. "Not really."

Emily smiles. "Instead of bracing against it, I want you to relax into it. Like you're getting into a hot tub. Just ease in. Can you try that?"

Julia concentrates.

Emily asks, "When you relax into it, does it change in any way?"

Julia breathed slowly. "It gets a little bigger when I stop fighting it."

"Good. Now send some gratitude to it. I know that sounds strange." Emily's voice was easy, not dramatic. "It's here because it has something for you. Can you thank it for showing up?"

Julia was quiet.

"When you do that, does it get bigger, smaller, or stay the same?"

"Smaller," she said. "Just a little."

Emily waited. "Now we're going to hand it a microphone. Like a little karaoke mic, so you can turn the volume up if you need to. We're going to ask it: what do you have for me about 'I don't have what it takes'? And I want you to just notice what floats through your mind. It might be a word. It might be an image. It might be a memory. It might be nothing, and that's okay too. But ask it, and tell me what comes up."

Silence.

Julia's brow shifted. Something crossed her face.

"There's a kitchen," she said slowly. "Not this one. My mom's kitchen."

"Stay with it." Emily didn't move. "What's happening in the kitchen?"

"I'm maybe twelve. Thirteen." Julia's voice went quieter. "My sister Mary is doing homework at the table. She's two years older. She always had everything organized. Color-coded folders. A plan." A small smile. "I'm making something. Cookies, I think. I always wanted to be in the kitchen."

"What happens in your body when you go back to that memory?"

Julia was quiet. "Like I was in the right place. Like this was mine." Then: "And also like the other stuff was hers."

"What was the other stuff?"

"The organized stuff. The plan. Knowing what came next." A pause. "Mary always knew what came next."

"How did you know that was hers and not yours?"

"My parents introduced us that way." Julia's voice stayed even. "Every teacher, every neighbor, every family friend. This is Mary, she's our driven one. And this is Julia, she's our creative one."

Emily didn't say anything.

"It wasn't bad. Mary wasn't mean about it. My parents weren't either." Julia looked slightly away from the camera. "It was just what was true. We were both just doing what we were good at."

"And what happened to the parts you weren't supposed to be good at?"

Julia was quiet for a long time.

"I just let Mary handle them," she said finally. "And then later I let Marcus handle them." She stopped. Her eyes opened.

She looked at Emily.

"Oh," she said quietly.

Emily didn't fill the silence.

Julia looked at her hands. "Marcus was the driven one. I was the creative one." She said it slowly, like she was reading something she had written a long time ago and forgotten. "It was the same deal."

"Yes," Emily said.

"And when he left…"

"You lost the person who handled the half you weren't supposed to be good at."

Julia's jaw tightened slightly. Not emotion exactly. Recognition.

"And you decided that proved it," Emily said quietly.

"That I was never enough on my own," Julia said it the way someone says something they've known for a while but never said out loud.

Neither of them spoke.

"Here's what I want you to notice," Emily said. "You have been running this bakery alone for a year. The lavender shortbread sold out by nine this morning. The law firm on Fifth has had a standing order for four years. A woman drove forty minutes last week because her daughter mentioned your cardamom brioche at a dinner party."

Julia looked at her.

"That's not someone who doesn't have what it takes," Emily said. "That's someone who decided she didn't."

Julia was quiet.

"The family story was just a story," Emily said. "It wasn't a verdict. Mary got the organized folder. You got the kitchen. But nobody said you couldn't have both. Twelve-year-old Julia just didn't know that yet."

Julia's face changed before she did. Not resolution. Just something loosening.

"Notice what's happening in your stomach right now," Emily said.

Julia checked in. "It's still there. But it's different. It's…" She paused. "Warmer."

"Good. That's it, starting to update." "Now say it. I have what it takes. Don't perform it. Just say it and notice what your body does."

Julia breathed in. "I have what it takes."

She was quiet.

"It doesn't feel completely true yet," she said. "But it doesn't feel as wrong as it did an hour ago."

"That's right," Emily said. "It's not supposed to feel true today. That's not how this works. You say it. You say it again. Your body starts paying attention. And every morning you show up at four-thirty and make something, you're giving that twelve-year-old a different story. That's the work."

Julia looked at her mug.

"Okay," she said quietly.

"Your homework," Emily said, "is simple. Once a day, say it out loud. I have what it takes. Not in your head. Out loud. Notice what sensation comes. Notice where it lives in your body. Don't try to fix it. Just observe it the way we did today."

Julia nodded.

"And one more thing." Emily's voice was warm but direct. "The next time you look at a spreadsheet or a supplier contract or anything that used to be Marcus's half, I want you to notice the thought that comes. Just notice it. Don't argue with it. Just bring it back next session."

"Okay," Julia said it like she meant it.

"Good work today," Emily said. "Seriously."

They said goodbye. The screen went dark.

Julia sat for a moment in the quiet of the bakery. The display cases were still dark. The kitchen smelled faintly of the morning's baking.

She thought about her mother's kitchen. Mary at the table with her color-coded folders. Herself at the counter making something she couldn't stop thinking about.

She had always thought the kitchen was the consolation prize.

She picked up her mug. Drank the last of the cold coffee.

Then she went to the back office, sat down at the desk, and opened the spreadsheet she had been avoiding for three days.

She didn't understand it all yet.

But she opened it.

She knew the road ahead won't be easy, but for the first time in a long while, she felt a glimmer of hope.

CHAPTER 9

How Did We Get Here?

Happy Tuesday

The bell above the door was the first thing Roman noticed. Small, brass, the kind of thing that had probably been there since the original owner.

He stepped inside. The smell hit before anything else did -- warm bread, something with cinnamon, coffee from the machine behind the counter. He stood just inside the door for a moment, which was not a thing he typically did.

Julia looked up from behind the counter. She registered him with a quick, genuine smile, the kind that didn't require preparation. "Roman. Hey."

"Hey." He moved toward the counter. "I need to order a cake."

She pulled a small notepad from her apron pocket. "What's the occasion?"

He paused. "No occasion. It's for my son, Andrew. I just thought..." He stopped. Tried again. "I wanted to do something. He's had a hard couple of weeks."

Julia set the pen down. "How old?"

"Thirteen."

"Chocolate?"

Roman almost smiled. "Is it that obvious?"

"It's always chocolate at thirteen." She leaned on the counter slightly. "Dark or milk?"

"Dark. He's past the dinosaur phase."

"Good. How about a chocolate cake, mocha buttercream, and dark chocolate shavings? Simple but not juvenile."

"That's exactly right," Roman said. He hadn't known what he wanted until she said it.

Julia wrote it down. "When do you need it?"

"Tomorrow, if that works."

"It works." She looked up at him. "He'll like it."

Roman nodded. He should have turned toward the door at that point. He didn't, quite. He looked at the display case for a moment, at the croissants lined up in a row, at the small card that said *Almond, Plain, Chocolate*. Everything labeled. Everything in its place.

"How are you doing?" he asked. Not the reflexive version of the question. The actual one.

Julia considered it honestly, which he appreciated. "Better than last month. I used one of Marcus's spreadsheets yesterday, and I didn't feel like I had to apologize to it." A small pause. "Which sounds ridiculous."

"It doesn't," Roman said.

She looked at him. "You doing okay?"

He thought about Andrew, who had been surprised by the idea of a cake, who had said, "A cake for what?" And then, when Roman said, "For Tuesday," he had laughed in a way Roman hadn't heard in a while. "Better than last month," he said.

Julia smiled. It was a quiet one. "Same time tomorrow for the pickup?"

"Same time tomorrow."

He turned toward the door. The bell rang again as he pushed it open, somehow smaller from this side.

"Roman."

He paused.

"Happy Tuesday," Julia said.

He held the door for a second. "Happy Tuesday."

He let it close behind him.

How did we get here?

The room felt different. Not the room. The people in it.

Emily arrived first, as she always did. She poured water, set her folder at the head of the table, and noted the small ways things had shifted. The chairs were already spread slightly wider, no longer bunched at one end.

Jade's sketchbook was open before Emily had finished settling. Theodore arrived without hurry, straightened his cuffs before he sat, his thumb finding the edge of his watch and stilling there. Cameron had a coffee and a pencil and the contained energy of someone who had already logged several hours before the rest of the world had started.

Julia came in last. Her bun was slightly looser than it had been at the first session. She walked straight to her seat and set her coffee down without the smile-at-everyone entrance she'd had the first time. Something had settled in her.

Roman arrived between Theodore and Julia. He said nothing when he came in, looked at the table the way he might review a set of plans, and chose his chair.

Emily waited until they had all settled.

"Before we talk about what's possible," she said, "I want to spend some time on what's automatic. Most of you didn't come here to work on yourselves. You came because something in your business isn't moving the way it should. And somewhere in the back of your mind, you've started to wonder if you're the variable."

She looked around the table.

"You probably have a list. Things you keep doing that you wish you didn't. Patterns you keep seeing in yourself. Some of them you've been trying to stop for years."

"They're not choices. They're responses. And until you understand what they're responding to, they're not going anywhere."

She moved forward without ceremony.

"Close your eyes if you're willing."

Theodore closed his eyes without hesitation, as if the instruction was a small relief. Jade followed. Roman watched the others for a moment, then let his close partway.

"You get a text," Emily said. "Someone who matters. Your most important client, your business partner, or a family member. It just says: Call me. Now. Marked urgent." She looked around the table. "Notice what's happening in your body right now."

The room was quiet.

Cameron went first. "My chest got tighter. Like bracing for something."

"I started making a list," Julia said. "Things I'd need to handle."

Theodore took a moment before he answered. "I felt heavier. Like something sat on my shoulders."

Jade's answer came quietly. "I assumed it was bad news. That I'd done something wrong."

Roman hadn't looked up from the table. "I started composing a response. Before I knew what the message said."

Emily nodded once.

"You just described five different nervous systems doing exactly what they were designed to do," she said. "None of that is a personality flaw. Those are survival strategies."

She paused.

"If you've seen *Inside Out*, you already have the map. Those weren't arbitrary characters. Each one in the control room had a specific job, a reason to be there. Your nervous system runs the same operation. Every response, every voice, every pattern we're going to work with: think of them as members of your inner board of directors. They've held their seats for a long time. They were appointed before any of you had an actual board to answer to. And they are very good at the jobs they were given."

She wrote three words on the board.

Fight. Flight. Freeze.

"These are your three primary responses to perceived threat. I say perceived because your nervous system doesn't always distinguish between a genuinely dangerous situation and one that only feels that way. It responds to the signal, not the reality."

She described each briefly.

"Fight moves toward the threat. Reclaims space. Wants control." A glance toward Cameron, who held it without flinching. "Flight moves away. Plans, pivots, creates distance. Wants options." Something in Julia's expression registered this without moving. "Freeze holds still. Analyzes, waits, conserves energy until there's more information." Roman didn't look up, but his jaw shifted slightly.

"These three are biological. Wired in." She paused. "There's a fourth response, but it's different. It's learned. When the environment made fighting back dangerous, and leaving wasn't an option, some people learned to accommodate. To move toward the person causing the harm and try to soften it. Make themselves useful. Agreeable. Safe to be around." She looked around the table. "We call it fawn. It isn't instinct. It's adaptation. It developed because at some point, it worked." Jade turned her bracelet once around her wrist.

"And when none of these resolve the threat, when the situation is sustained, and the system runs out of options, freeze can move into something quieter. We call it flop. The system going offline. It can look like resignation. Like not caring. Like not bothering to try."

Theodore's gaze stayed on the table. His thumb moved once to the edge of his watch.

"These aren't pathological," Emily said. "They're adaptive. And they were formed long before any of you were running businesses, managing teams, or trying to connect with your teenagers."

She gave them a second scenario. Sharper.

"You're presenting something you've worked on for weeks. Someone in the room interrupts you. Talks over you like you hadn't spoken. Before you name anything, just notice."

Cameron answered without pausing. "I'd cut back in. Keep my voice even, but I'd take the floor back."

Emily nodded. "Fight. Reclaims space without necessarily escalating."

Julia's answer came more slowly. "I'd probably let it go. Tell myself it wasn't worth the energy." She looked at the table. "And then spend the rest of the meeting annoyed at myself for not saying anything."

"Flight," Emily said. "But it rarely feels like retreat. It usually feels like strategy. That's what makes it hard to catch."

Julia's jaw tightened slightly. Yes.

Theodore was quiet for a moment. Then: "I'd feel like whatever I said next wouldn't matter. Not angry. Just tired."

"That's further than freeze," Emily said. "Freeze is still waiting. Still gathering information. What you're describing is the system deciding the effort won't change the outcome, so it stops spending the energy." She looked at him. "We call it flop. It's not apathy. It's a system that ran out of road."

Theodore didn't look up. But something in his expression shifted, a word settling into the right place after years of not quite having one.

Jade spoke carefully. "I'd assume I'd done something to cause it. I'd probably find a way to check in with them privately afterward. Make sure we were still okay."

"Fawn," Emily said. "Safety through repair."

Roman had been quiet. His answer, when it came, was measured. "I'd draft something in my head. The thing I should have said. Revise it. Let it sit. Then decide whether to say it at all."

"There's freeze in that," Emily said. "And controlled fight underneath it. The energy is there. You're deciding where it goes."

Roman looked at her steadily. "Yes."

"Here's what I want you to understand about every one of these," Emily said, moving back toward the center of the room. "They worked. Every single one of them worked at some point in your life."

She folded her hands.

"They helped you manage situations when you didn't have the skills or the size or the resources to manage them differently. They helped you stay close to the people you depended on. They helped you stay functional when the environment wasn't safe."

She paused.

"Mission accomplished."

Something in the room shifted. Quiet, but real.

"But the nervous system isn't a storyteller. It's a pattern-matcher. It learned what worked once, and it applies that pattern wherever it detects a similar signal. Which is why you can walk into a boardroom, or a performance review, or a difficult conversation with someone you love, and find yourself responding the way you did at eleven years old."

Julia looked at the table. Her hands went still.

"The pattern isn't irrational," Emily said. "It just isn't updated."

She gave it a second, then moved to the board. She picked up the marker and wrote. Not a list. Just a phrase.

I'm not enough.

"Every belief we'll work through in this group is a chapter of the same story. I'm not capable enough. I'm not worthy enough. I'm not valuable enough. I'm not lovable enough. The words vary." She set the marker down. "But underneath almost all of them there's one sentence your nervous system wrote a long time ago."

She looked at the board.

"It isn't true. But it feels true because your body has been responding as though it is for years. And the body is very convincing."

"When something frightened or hurt you as a child," Emily continued, "your body reacted. That reaction is what we call an emotion, and the word itself is worth paying attention to. E-motion. Energy designed to move. Your heart rate climbed. Your muscles tightened. Energy surged. All of it meant to discharge through movement, crying, shaking, talking, or running. Something physical to let the activation complete its cycle and return to baseline."

She looked around the table.

"Take something almost everyone has experienced. You're a kid. You say something in class, get the answer wrong, make a joke at the wrong moment, whatever it was. The room laughs. Not with you. At you. Your face goes hot. Your chest tightens. Your stomach drops. That energy is real. Your body is trying to protect you. But you're eleven, and you're in a classroom, and there's nowhere for it to go. You can't run. You can't cry. So you sit there and hold it, and the activation doesn't complete."

She paused.

"Some people decide in that moment: never again. Don't volunteer, don't risk it, stay quiet. The nervous system files it away: this is what happens when you put yourself out there."

She let it breathe.

"Other people make the exact opposite decision. They become the class clown. They take control of the joke before anyone else can. Same experience. Same sensation. Completely different strategy. Others have a more secure home life, and they may tell their parents and never think about it again."

"If you grew up in a family where physically releasing the activation wasn't welcome in any form. Someone said, "Stop crying, or I'll give you something to cry about." Or you had to pretend like everything was perfect so your parents didn't look bad. Or there was no one there to help you process it." She paused. "So the activation didn't complete. It got stored."

She gave them a moment.

"Think of it like a beach ball you're holding underwater. You can hold it down for a long time. But it doesn't disappear, and eventually, at the least convenient moment, it surfaces." Her voice stayed even. "The boardroom. The dinner table. The conversation you thought you were fully prepared for."

Cameron's hands had gone still on the table.

"Over time, the stored activation became a shortcut. Your nervous system started forming beliefs based on what the incomplete experience taught it. This kind of situation isn't safe.

This is what happens when I speak up. This is what love costs. Not a conclusion your rational mind reached. The meaning your nervous system assigned from incomplete data, under duress, at an age when you couldn't contextualize it."

She paused.

"Children are magnificent meaning-making machines. When something goes wrong, when a parent withdraws, when you're overlooked, when the room makes you feel invisible or too much at once, the child doesn't say, 'This environment is limited and imperfect.' The child says, 'There must be something wrong with me.' Because it's more manageable, if it's about you, you can fix it. You can try harder. You can be better."

She paused.

"That conclusion goes into the filing cabinet. Not as a thought. As a threat. The nervous system logs it as information about what's dangerous. And because the child's brain doesn't yet have the processing power to evaluate whether the filing is accurate, the file stays. The inner critic becomes its manager. Its job is to pull that file every time a situation feels similar, to make sure you never forget what you learned about staying safe." She paused. "Over time, what started as a child's best guess at making sense of pain becomes a belief. Not because it was ever true. Because it was filed, and confirmed, and filed again."

Theodore's eyes came up from the table. He said nothing, but he was present in a way he sometimes wasn't.

"The problem isn't that your brain formed those beliefs," Emily said. "The problem is that the body never got to finish what it started. So the shortcut remains, even when the original situation is decades behind you."

Julia was the one who broke the quiet. "So what do we do with all of this? I mean, I've always thought the answer was to counterbalance it. Focus on the good. Positive thinking. Just... outweigh the negative."

Emily nodded once. "That's usually where people go first. And sometimes it helps. For a while." She paused. "But it doesn't touch what's underneath. The loop is still open. The beach ball is still down there."

She moved to the edge of the room.

"What we do instead is go back and finish what we didn't finish."

Jade leaned forward. "So how far back does this go? Are we going to be working through everything that's ever happened?"

"We're working with what's active right now," Emily said. "We're not excavating your entire past. The nervous system learns from the present. Not from the archive."

Jade settled back slightly.

"Most of you have a voice that monitors your performance," Emily said. "It knows when you've made a mistake before you've finished making it. It has opinions about your decisions, your capacity, how you're showing up."

She looked around the table.

"Remember the board of directors. This voice isn't just a member. It's the board chair. It's been the chair for a long time, and if we're being honest, it's been a bit of a dictator."

She paused.

"Back to that control panel from *Inside Out*. Joy gets pulled from headquarters, and suddenly fear, anger, and disgust are running things. For most of us, that happened often enough, and stayed long enough, that something new moved in and took the chair."

"We call it the inner critic. And here's what most people get wrong about it. It didn't move in to hurt you. It moved in to protect you. It learned that staying small kept you safer. That being hard on yourself before someone else could be was better than being caught off guard. That managing everyone else's reactions was easier than sitting with your own."

"It worked. In the environment it was designed for."

"But it's still there. Still running a protection strategy built for an eleven-year-old. In your boardroom. In your marriage. In every room where you're trying to lead."

Cameron looked up.

Emily held her gaze. "What does yours say when you think about easing up?"

The answer was immediate. Cameron's voice was flatter than usual. "That I'll fall behind. Things will slip. That I'll drop something I can't afford to drop."

"And what is it protecting?"

A longer pause.

"Proving everyone right who said this was a mistake."

"Your inner critic believes pressure equals protection," Emily said. "And it's probably been right. Up to a point." She looked around the circle. "Here's what I know about every one of them: they have been working hard. They've been watching out for you. Every time yours said you weren't enough, every time it woke you up at three in the morning, every time it sent you right back in when you needed to stop, it thought it was keeping you safe."

The room was quiet.

"So we don't fight it. We don't try to kick it off the board. It will fight back, and it will win, because your brain's survival wiring will override your best intentions every time." She let that land. "Instead, we thank it. We say, 'you've done good work. You've kept me safe.' And then we ask it to step out of the chair. Not off the board. Just out of the chair."

She looked at each of them.

"Because Adult You is ready to run this meeting now. The version of you who can make decisions based on facts and feelings. Based on what protected you then and what's actually true now."

The room sat with that.

"Today wasn't about fixing anything," Emily said. "It was about understanding what the body was protecting. And why your nervous system built the system it did."

She let that be enough.

"This work isn't about becoming someone new. It's about stepping into the chair that was always yours."

She looked at each of them.

"One practice before we meet again. When you notice the inner critic in the board chair, and you will, don't fight it. Don't try to silence it. Just notice it's there." She paused. "Thank it. You can do it silently. It sounds strange, but try it. 'Thank you. I know you've been trying to protect me.' And then: 'I've got it from here.'"

A few quiet nods.

"You're not removing it. You're just stepping into the chair."

Emily's last words to the room were practical. "If your next individual session isn't on the calendar, get it there. The group work opens the pattern. The one-on-one is where we make it personal."

Chairs shifted. A few quiet conversations started. No one rushed toward the door.

Roman walked out, staring at his phone. Andrew had texted him at some point during the session, a single line: what kind of icing is on the cake?

Roman typed back: Mocha. You'll like it.

Three dots appeared, then disappeared, then appeared again.

okay

Roman put his phone in his pocket and walked out.

• • •

Theodore was the last to stand. He pressed his thumb once against the face of his watch, the way he always did when he was thinking, then let his hand drop. He straightened his jacket with the same deliberate care and moved toward the door without speaking to anyone.

At the door, he stopped, just for a second.

Then he left.

CHAPTER 10

Theodore, The Painting Under the Varnish

Theodore joined from his workshop. He was already there when Emily connected, seated at his workbench with the particular stillness of someone who had been sitting quietly for a while before the call began. Behind him, the shelves held their familiar arrangement of frames and covered canvases. His father's lamp threw its circle of warm light over his left shoulder.

"Theodore," Emily said.

"Emily." He nodded once.

"How was the week?"

He considered the question without rushing. "Evan came by on Thursday. He stayed longer than usual." The corner of his mouth moved slightly. "He brought coffee. Which means he wanted something."

Emily smiled. "Wonder where he got that."

Theodore looked at her for a moment. "Yes," he said. "I've thought about that."

He set his hands flat on the workbench. "He has a client. The furniture company I mentioned. They sell vintage-inspired reproductions." He said it without editorializing. "They want me to consult on their marketing campaign. Be the face of authentic craftsmanship, is how Evan described it."

"How did that land?"

Theodore was quiet for a moment. "I haven't given him an answer."

"How long ago did he ask?"

"Tuesday."

Emily let that sit. Then: "Let's look at your numbers."

She walked him through the assessment. Theodore studied the two columns with the focused attention he brought to a damaged canvas. His restoration work domain was solid. Eights across the board.

His business domain told a different story. Emily let him look at it without explaining it.

"What do you notice?" she asked.

Theodore studied the gap for a moment. "I am valuable," he said. "There's a significant difference between the two."

"What do you make of that?"

He looked at the number for the business domain. A four. "The work has value," he said carefully. "I know that."

"And yet."

He didn't finish the sentence either.

Emily waited. When it became clear he wasn't going to continue, she said, "We'll start there. But first, I want to activate it a little."

Theodore looked at her. A trace of wariness.

"I want you to imagine something," Emily said. "You call Evan back. You say yes to the furniture company. Next Thursday, you drive to their offices. You walk into a conference room. There are four people around the table. Marketing team. They've never heard of Sinclair Restorations. They know the word craftsmanship, but they've never watched someone actually restore a piece. They need you to make their reproductions feel real." She paused. "You sit down. They're looking at you. What happens in your body right now as you picture that?"

Theodore was quiet.

"Take a moment," Emily said. "Don't think about it. Just notice what's happening physically. Typically, people notice something in their throat, chest, or stomach."

A pause.

"There's something in my chest," he said finally.

"Okay. Where exactly?"

"Upper chest. Just below the collarbone."

"Good. Is it tight? Pulling? Pushing? What is it doing?"

Theodore considered. "Pressing. Inward."

"How big of an area?"

He scanned. "Not large."

"Okay. Stay with it. Don't try to get rid of it. We're just going to observe it." Emily's voice was steady. "Does it have a shape? It may not."

A long pause. Longer than most people would take.

"I'm not sure," Theodore said.

"That's fine. Let's keep looking. Zoom in on it like you're examining a piece up close. Walk all around it. Does anything come?"

Another pause.

"It might be flat," he said. "Like a panel. But I'm not certain."

"Okay. A flat panel. Is there any temperature to it? Hot, cold, or body temperature?"

"Cool," he said. "Cooler than the rest."

"Does it have a color? It may not."

Theodore was quiet for longer than the previous questions.

"Dark," he said. "Brown, maybe. Hard to say."

"That's fine. I want you to zoom in even closer. Like you're right up against it. Is there anything about the surface? A texture? It may not be there."

A longer pause.

"Grain," he said quietly. He seemed mildly surprised by this. "Like wood grain. Very fine. Under something."

"Under something."

"Like it's been coated," he said. "You'd have to look closely to see it."

Emily let that sit for a moment before continuing. "Okay. We have a cool, dark panel. Flat. With grain underneath something. I just want you to observe it. Like a piece that just came into the shop. You're not going to work on it yet. Just look at it."

Theodore's expression shifted slightly. This was language he understood.

"Does it change at all when you observe it that way?"

"It settles," he said after a moment. "It was pressing before. Now it's just there."

"Good. Now I want you to relax into it. Like a hot tub. Just allow it to be there without bracing against it. Does it get bigger, smaller, or stay the same?"

Theodore was quiet, working with it. "Same," he said. "But less insistent."

"Good. Now I want you to feel some gratitude for it. I know that sounds strange." Emily's voice was easy, not dramatic. "This panel has been in your chest for a while. It's here to give you something. Can you just thank it for being there?"

A long pause. Theodore's thumb moved to the edge of his watchband and stilled.

"Yes," he said finally.

"Does it change when you do that?"

"Slightly warmer." He reported it like a temperature reading. "Just slightly."

"Good. Now we're going to hand it a microphone. Like the karaoke machines. We're going to turn it up and ask it: what have you got for me? Just notice what floats through your mind. It might be a word. Might be an image. A story may come to mind. Might be nothing yet. Just tell me what comes."

Silence.

A long silence. The kind Theodore was comfortable with, and most people weren't.

Emily waited.

Theodore's brow shifted. A flicker crossed his face.

"What's coming up?" Emily asked softly.

"I expected my father," Theodore said.

Emily waited.

"It wasn't my father."

Another pause.

"It was Marianne," he said. He said it the way he would report a measurement. Flat and precise. "She's standing in the kitchen. Just standing there." He paused. "She said something to me last week. She said I talk to my workbench more than I talk to her." He delivered this the same way. Just the fact of it. "I didn't know what to say to that."

Emily held the silence.

"What's happening in your chest right now?" she asked. "The panel."

Theodore checked in. "It's different," he said. "The grain is more visible."

"Like some of the coating came off."

"Yes."

Neither of them spoke for a moment.

"My father and I didn't need words," Theodore said. "We worked. That was the language. He would hand me a tool I hadn't asked for yet because he knew what I needed before I did." His thumb moved along the watchband. "Everything was understood."

"Yes," Emily said.

"Marianne needs the words."

He said it exactly the same way he said everything else. But it landed differently.

Emily looked at him carefully. "How long have you known that?"

"A while," he said.

She didn't push it further. "Here's what I want you to notice," Emily said. "You walked into that conference room in your imagination, strangers who have never seen the work, and your body gave you a panel with grain hidden underneath a coating." She paused. "Your body knows what's underneath. It always has. That's what thirty years of this work have built."

Theodore was quiet.

"The question isn't whether the work is valuable," Emily said. "Your body already answered that. The question is whether you can let the grain show. In that conference room. At home." She paused. "Those aren't that different."

Theodore looked toward the lamp for a long moment.

"That's a different kind of restoration," he said quietly.

"It is." She didn't move past it. "When did you last tell Marianne something instead of showing her?"

Theodore was quiet.

"Not a gesture. A sentence."

"I don't know," he said finally. "It's been a while."

"What would happen if you said it tonight?"

He considered that. "She'd probably think something was wrong."

"Because words from you are so rare, they read as emergencies."

Theodore didn't answer. That was its own answer.

"Here's what I want you to do this week," Emily said. "Once a day, before you start any work, before you touch anything in the shop, I want you to say out loud: I am valuable. Not because of what I'm about to make. Not because of what I finished yesterday." She looked at him. "Just that."

He was quiet.

"Do it now."

A long moment. Then, quietly: "I am valuable."

"Again."

"I am valuable."

Something in his face moved. Not relief. Something more careful than that. Like a door he hadn't opened in a long time and wasn't sure yet what was on the other side.

"And one more thing," Emily said. Her voice was direct but easy. "Say one thing to Marianne this week that you would normally just show her. Not a gesture. A sentence." She paused. "It doesn't have to be much. It just has to be words."

Theodore looked at her for a moment.

"All right," he said.

"Good work today," Emily said. "I mean that."

They said goodbye. The screen went dark.

Theodore sat for a moment in the quiet of the workshop. Around him, the pieces held their places on the shelves. The frames. The covered canvases. The tools along the wall.

He looked at his hands on the workbench. He didn't pick anything up.

"I am valuable."

His voice in the empty workshop was quieter than he expected.

He sat with that for a moment. Then he went to find Marianne.

The Photographs

The shop was quiet when Evan came in.

Theodore was at the workbench, fitting a drawer that had warped slightly over the course of a century. He heard the bell above the door and didn't look up.

"I was in the area," Evan said.

"I know." Theodore meant it factually. Evan's office was six blocks away. He had always been in the area.

Evan came to the bench and looked at the drawer. He had inherited Theodore's way of looking at things quietly before speaking, which Theodore had never thought about until now.

"How's the piece?"

"Getting there."

Evan put his hands in his pockets. He looked around the shop the way he always did, slowly, like he was reading something he'd read before but found new things in.

"I have the mockup, if you want to look at it again."

Theodore kept his hands on the drawer. He'd looked at it twice before and found reasons to change the subject both times. The second time, he had redirected with a question about Evan's drive, which was so transparent that Evan went quiet for the rest of the visit.

"Show me the photograph section," Theodore said.

Evan was still for a moment. He took out his phone and set it on the bench.

The photographs were arranged in pairs. Before and after. A chair with a collapsed seat beside the same chair restored, the finish brought back from gray. A cabinet door split down the center, then whole, the grain matched so precisely that the repair was invisible unless you knew where to look. A mirror with its original glass re-silvered, the image in it clear again after eighty years of clouding.

Theodore looked at them without picking up the phone. Steadily, without rushing. The way he looked at a piece he was assessing.

"Who took these?" he asked.

"I did. Last time I was here."

Theodore looked at the cabinet pair. He had spent eleven days on that repair. He remembered the afternoon he matched the grain.

"The light is good," he said. "In the before photograph. It shows what it actually was." He looked at the after. "And what it became."

He looked at a few more. He didn't say anything else for a while. Evan didn't either.

When Theodore set down the chisel and picked up the phone to look more closely, Evan stayed where he was and let him.

CHAPTER 11

The Belief Underneath

Saturday Morning

Cameron's stall was easy to spot.

It was organized the way Cameron organized things, with the efficiency of someone who had thought through the layout before she arrived. Produce arranged by size, signs handwritten in the same clean capitals, a small laminated card propped next to a certificate from the regional agricultural board.

Jade almost walked past it.

She moved through markets slowly. Not looking for anything specific. Just letting things come. She noticed texture before she noticed price. She had already passed three stalls and spent eight dollars on honey when she recognized the back of Cameron's head.

Cameron was bagging something for a customer and didn't see her.

Jade waited. She looked at the laminated card. Regenerative Certification. Three years, Cameron had said in the session. She'd been working toward it for three years.

The customer left. Cameron turned, registered brief surprise, and shifted into something efficient and warm. "Hey. I didn't know you came to this market."

"I usually go to the one near my studio," Jade said. "I had an appointment nearby."

Cameron was already straightening a row of things that didn't need straightening. "Looking for anything specific?"

"No, just waiting for something to catch my eye." Jade looked at the table. A small basket held something pale and knobby she didn't recognize. "What's this?"

"Celeriac. Most people don't know what to do with it."

"What do you do with it?"

"Roast it, mostly. It's better than it looks."

Jade picked one up and turned it over. The weight was satisfying in a way she would have had trouble explaining. She set it back down. "I saw the Certified Organic card. Congratulations."

Cameron glanced at it. "Thanks. Took long enough." Her eyes were already moving to something down the row.

"Are you doing anything to celebrate?"

Cameron's eyes came back. "I'm here," she said. And then, as if she'd heard herself: "I mean, I'll probably do something when the next phase is finished."

Before Jade could respond, a man stopped at the stall. He didn't look at the produce. He looked at Cameron.

"Hey." Bruce said it the way people say it when they've been looking forward to the saying.

Cameron straightened. Something in her shifted, small and fast, and then went back to efficient. "Hey. I'm working."

"I know you're working." He put his hands in his pockets. He didn't seem bothered by the response. "I just wanted to ask if you'd eaten. There's a place down two rows."

"I ate at four-thirty."

"That doesn't count as eating."

A customer came up beside Jade, and Cameron turned to them with the clean, practiced warmth she used with everyone. The man waited. When Cameron handed over the bag and the customer moved on, he was still there.

"I'll find you at noon," he said. Not a question.

"I might be busy at noon."

He smiled at that, like it was something he'd heard before and didn't mind. He nodded once at Jade, a brief acknowledgment, and moved off down the row without hurrying.

Cameron watched him go for a moment and then looked back at the table.

Jade bought the celeriac and a bunch of something leafy she also didn't entirely recognize.

"See you Tuesday," Cameron said, already turning.

Jade walked back down the row. She thought about the laminated card sitting between the root vegetables and the greens. Three years of work, and Cameron was already on to the next thing.

She wondered if Cameron even noticed.

She thought about the man moving casually down the row. She wondered if Cameron had noticed that either.

The Belief Underneath

Cameron had moved her chair before Emily got there.

Jade and Julia arrived mid-conversation, the way they always did now, voices dropping as they crossed the threshold. Theodore placed his coat over the back of his chair with the same deliberate ease he brought to everything. Roman was on time to the minute.

Emily set her folder down. She let them settle.

"Last session," she said, "I asked you to notice when the inner critic stepped into the board chair. And to try, once if you could, to thank it for what it's been protecting, and see what happened if you took the seat instead." She looked around the circle. "I'm curious what you found."

The silence was different from what it had been six weeks ago. Not reluctant. Just real.

Cameron set her coffee cup down with more precision than the gesture required.

"I tried. I was up before five on Thursday." She looked at the table. "The regenerative certification came through. I've been working toward it for three years. I had about twenty minutes of actually feeling good about it. Then the critic stepped in with the list of what it didn't fix yet."

"What did you do?"

"I said it out loud. It was just the dogs and me. 'Thank you. I know what you're protecting.'" She paused. "Felt ridiculous. The list didn't stop. But I finished my coffee before I started writing it down. For me, that's something."

Jade turned her bracelet once around her wrist. "Mine was in the studio. Late, before the trunk show. I'd been remaking a piece I'd already made, one that sold well the last time." She looked at her hands. "I kept going back in. Adjusting things already finished."

"What did you do when you noticed it?"

"I put my tools down." She was quiet for a moment. "I didn't say it the way we talked about in here. I just sat and looked at the piece. Tried to figure out what I was actually afraid of." She looked up. "I think I was afraid they'd see the whole collection and decide that's as good as it gets for me."

"Did you step back into the chair?"

"I stopped changing the piece." She looked at her hands again. "I think that's the same thing."

Emily held that. "It is."

Jade nodded once. Her eyes moved to the others before she'd decided to look. Cameron was studying the table. Julia had both hands around her water glass. A quick read of the room, the kind she'd been catching herself doing for weeks now.

She looked back at her own hands.

Julia had been listening with her hands around her water glass. "A wholesale buyer came into the bakery last week. Wanted to talk about carrying our bread at a restaurant group." She exhaled slowly. "The timing was terrible. We're already at capacity. Taking it on right now would mean doing it badly."

"What did you do?"

"I said I'd figure it out." Her voice was careful. "And then spent four days trying to figure out how to make it work." She looked up briefly. "I never tried the practice. I just ran the numbers until I ran out of numbers to run."

"What would the critic have said if you'd turned it down?"

"That they'd think I wasn't serious. That someone who had it together would find a way. That I'd lose the chance and deserve to."

Theodore turned his watch once around his wrist. "Evan called. I let it go to voicemail." He looked at the table. "I sat with my hands on a piece I'd been working on and tried to pay attention to what was happening in my body while I watched his name on the screen."

"What was happening?"

"It was tight." He considered the word carefully. "Like something was defending something."

"Like something needed to be kept safe," Emily said.

His gaze came up slowly. A single nod, barely perceptible.

She held that a moment, then looked at Roman.

Roman had been still through all of it. He chose his words with the care of someone who had learned to measure the ones he picked.

"Andrew told me again he wants to quit baseball and do theater." He looked at the table. "I caught myself about to redirect him. Give him a responsible reason to finish the season." He looked up. "I didn't."

"What did you do instead?"

"I asked him what kind of play." His face showed the emotion, not quite pride but pointed in that direction. "He talked for twenty minutes. I had no idea he had so many opinions about anything. He wants to do something with words. I didn't know."

The room was still for a moment.

Emily looked around the circle.

"You all caught it," she said. "Cameron, before the list started. Jade, before you went back in. Julia, you didn't do the practice, but you knew exactly what the critic was protecting. Theodore, you felt it in your body before you made a decision. Roman, you caught yourself and asked a different question instead." She paused. "Most people are halfway through the reaction before they even realize the critic was driving. You saw it. That's what we've been building."

She stood and walked to the board. She uncapped the marker.

"I want to show you what's actually happening when you do that. Imagine two film crews have been following you your entire life."

"One crew has been capturing every moment proving the negative belief true. Every rejection. Every time you tried and fell short. Every room that didn't make space for you, every relationship that ended, every goal that took longer than it should have. They have excellent footage. They've been at this since you were small.

"The other crew has been capturing every moment proving the positive belief true. Every time you figured something out under pressure. Every person who chose you. Every goal you met, every room you held, every time someone you respect looked at you and saw exactly what you hoped they'd see." She looked around the table. "They have excellent footage, too.

"Both crews have been filming the same life. They've just been pointing the camera at different things. And the negative crew isn't louder because it's more accurate. Your brain was built to scan for danger. Not because something is wrong with you, but because that's what kept humans alive."

Roman looked at the space in front of him, still absorbing.

"You know where the file came from. The child who decided 'there must be something wrong with me' wasn't wrong to file it. It was the most workable conclusion available at the time."

Julia looked up.

"The belief isn't a flaw in your thinking. It was a survival strategy. A framework for staying safe in an environment you couldn't leave." Emily scanned the room. "And it worked. You survived.

You tried harder. You built things. You got better. You're sitting in this room because the belief drove you here, in some form."

She paused.

"The cost is that the belief never stops driving you. One more achievement and then you'll feel like you're enough. One more milestone and you'll finally trust yourself. If someone with enough authority says you belong, you'll believe it. If your parents had said the right words, you'd feel lovable now."

Jade turned her bracelet once around her wrist. Stopped.

"The belief has convinced you that the proof has to come from outside. But the file is on the inside. It always was."

She let that sit for a moment.

"Have you ever watched the director's cut of a movie?" Emily said. "The director decides what gets cut and what gets kept. What defines the story?"

She looked around the table.

"The inner critic has been sitting in the director's chair. It's been deciding which footage matters, which reel tells the truth about who you are. Up until now, it's been the one deciding which screening room you're in. When it steps in, it takes you straight to the negative reel. Every time. Not because it wants to hurt you. Because it genuinely believes that footage is what's keeping you safe."

Emily set the marker down.

"I want you to try something." She looked around the table. "Think of a genuine win from the past few months. Something real, something finished. Not what's next, not what still needs work. Something that already happened." She paused. "Bring it to mind and notice what your body does."

The room was quiet.

Cameron thought of the certification. She was also already thinking about the next phase.

Julia held her water glass and thought of the bread account she'd landed in February, the one that had required her to rebuild the morning shift from scratch. She found something. It was small.

Theodore's eyes went to the far wall. He was thinking about a walnut cabinet he'd finished the previous week.

"Now," Emily said, "think about a moment in the last few months when something went wrong. When you made the wrong call, or someone looked at you with doubt, or something didn't hold the way it needed to."

She watched them.

"Notice the difference," she said.

Nobody spoke for a moment.

"The second one was faster," Jade said quietly.

Emily nodded. "It was."

She moved back toward the center of the room.

"You've already felt this. Not as a concept. Right now, in this room." She looked around the table. "There's a version of what just happened that you've probably heard before — maybe on a motivational poster somewhere. Beliefs become thoughts. Thoughts become words. Words become actions." She paused. "And for the positive reel, that chain holds. You bring the win to mind. Maybe you find something. Maybe it's a little distant."

She paused.

"But the negative moment didn't wait for thought. The sensation was already in your body before you'd finished remembering it. Not a character flaw — just the difference between a cycle that finished and one that didn't. The negative experience stored its charge in your body because the activation never completed. The positive crew filmed the same life, but filed the footage without the same physical weight behind it. That's why it doesn't register the same way."

She waited for it to sink in.

"But it was there. The positive crew has been filming your whole life. As you complete the cycles, the footage you thought was lost starts to become visible. Not because it's new. Because the path to that screening room finally opens."

"The work isn't to argue with the footage," Emily said. "It isn't to prove the negative crew wrong. It's to complete what never completed. When the cycle finishes, the door to the other screening room opens. But the footage couldn't register as real until the body got to finish what it started. Once it does, the two reels start to weigh the same."

She looked around the table.

"That's why you are the director. Not just the star. You get to decide what gets kept. What defines the story?"

Cameron exhaled. Not dramatically. Just a small, controlled release she probably hadn't authorized.

"Two new tools I want you to practice before we meet again," Emily said. "The first: when you catch the crew rolling, name it. Out loud if the moment allows, quietly if it doesn't. 'The crew is filming.' That's it. Don't argue with the footage. Don't try to replace it with something better. Just name it and notice where in your body you feel it."

She paused.

"The second: when something good happens, don't move past it. You'll want to. Notice that impulse." She looked at Cameron for just a moment, then away. "Then lean into it. Stay in it long enough for your body to actually feel it. Don't observe it from a distance. Amplify it."

Cameron spoke first. "Twenty minutes." She looked at the table. "The certification came through on Thursday. I had twenty minutes of actually feeling good about it before I was already writing the next list." She looked up. "I thought the good feeling was the problem. Like if I stayed in it, something would slip."

Jade looked at her sketchbook. Theodore's thumb found the edge of his watch.

Roman set his pen down. "What does completing a cycle actually look like? In practice." He looked at Emily. "Because I know what running the numbers looks like."

"That's what the one-on-one work is for," Emily said.

Theodore had been still through most of it. He said, without looking up: "I've been treating the positive footage like it was the one that wasn't accurate."

The room held it.

They stayed longer after this session than they had after the first two. Not because anyone called a meeting. Just because the room didn't immediately invite leaving.

Jade was already writing. Theodore sat at the table without watching anything in particular. Cameron had her phone out but wasn't looking at it.

Julia was the first to go. She stood at the door and looked back at the room for a moment: the table, the marker Emily had set down, the board. She took out her notebook and wrote something short. Not for anyone else. Just so she wouldn't lose it before she got to her car.

Then she walked out.

Roman paused at the door on his way out. He looked back at Theodore.

Not long. Just enough.

Theodore gave a single nod.

CHAPTER 12

Cameron, What She Built

As Emily logged into Zoom, Cameron was already waiting.

Emily gave her a warm smile. "How are you holding up, Cameron? How's everything going with the farm?"

Cameron shrugged, her expression hard to read. "The farm's fine. I mean, we're making progress. I've been focusing on the regenerative practices on those 20 acres, and it's been a lot of work, but I know it's the right direction. It's just... I'm tired."

Emily studied her. "Tired how?"

Cameron exhaled through her nose. "Like I'm constantly pushing. Constantly proving. If this doesn't work, it's on me. If it fails, it confirms what everyone already thinks."

"And what's that?" Emily asked gently.

"That I shouldn't be the one running it."

The words landed heavily between them.

Emily nodded. "When we did your assessment, when it comes to leading the farm, you rated yourself a four out of ten on 'I am worthy.'"

Cameron gave a tight smile. "That sounds about right."

"Notice," Emily said, steady, "that wasn't a score about competence. You didn't rate your skills. You rated your worthiness."

Cameron's jaw tightened.

"There's a difference between valuable and worthy," Emily continued. "Valuable is what you contribute. Worthy is whether you believe you deserve to be here before you contribute anything."

Cameron looked away.

"Worthy is not about output," Emily said. "It's not about acres converted. It's not about profit margins. It's not about whether your dad approves. Worthy is about this: are you allowed to exist as you are and be treated with dignity?"

Cameron swallowed.

"My dad wanted a son," she said quietly. "Naming me Cameron was his way of trying to get close. I've always known that. I just... figured I had to compensate."

Emily nodded slowly.

"That wasn't a performance critique," she said. "That was a rejection of form."

Cameron looked up.

"When rejection targets something you can't change—your gender, your temperament, your body—the brain doesn't interpret it as 'I need to try harder.' It interprets it as 'I am wrong.'"

Silence filled the screen.

"You weren't rejected for effort," Emily continued. "You were rejected for being."

Cameron's throat tightened.

"And when that happens," Emily said gently, "a person often spends their life trying to earn back something they never lost."

Cameron let out a slow breath.

"I'm so angry all the time," she admitted. "It's like fire in my chest. I feel like I have to fight to prove I deserve to be here."

"Of course you do," Emily said. "Anger makes sense when someone believes they have to defend their right to exist."

Cameron blinked.

"But here's the truth," Emily continued, her tone calm and firm. "Worthy is not earned. It's inherent. If you are breathing, you are worthy. Period."

Cameron stared at her.

"You don't earn dignity. You shouldn't have to earn belonging or love. You don't earn the right to lead your own life. Those are baseline human rights."

The fire in Cameron's chest flickered.

"The hard part is this—if you don't believe you're worthy apart from performance, you'll never feel done. No matter how successful the farm becomes."

That landed.

Cameron leaned back slightly. "So what do I do with the anger?"

"Let's listen to it," Emily said. "Close your eyes. When you think about not being worthy, about having to prove yourself, where do you feel it?"

Cameron closed her eyes. "My stomach. It's tight."

"Describe it."

"It's like a ball. Round but uneven. Like a water balloon."

"Temperature?"

"Hot. Like lava."

"Color?"

"Dark red."

"Stay with it," Emily said. "Zoom in."

Cameron's breathing deepened. "It's trembling underneath. Like it could burst."

"Zoom out."

"It's growing. Filling my torso."

"What happens if you don't fight it?"

Cameron paused. "It's turning solid."

"What shape?"

"A stone. Heavy. Jagged."

"Temperature now?"

"Colder. Almost black."

Emily nodded. "Good. Let it be there. Don't fix it. Just allow it."

Cameron sat with it.

After a moment, her shoulders dropped slightly.

"It's not attacking me anymore," she said. "It's just there."

"Thank it," Emily said. "This stone formed for a reason."

Cameron went still. Her jaw shifted once. Then nothing moved.

When she opened her eyes, the hardness was gone for a second, just a second, before she pulled herself back.

"It said something," she said.

"What did it say?"

"Precious."

Emily's expression shifted, but she didn't rush.

"Precious," she repeated. "Not productive. Not profitable. Not impressive."

Cameron's face relaxed. Not softness exactly. More like a wall that didn't know what to do when no one was pushing on it.

"That's not a word anyone's ever used for me," she said.

Emily nodded. "What does it do to you? Sitting with it right now."

Cameron looked at the wall to the left of her screen. Her jaw worked once.

"It makes me want to argue with it," she said finally.

"I know," Emily said. "What would you argue?"

"That it's not useful." A pause. "That precious doesn't run a farm."

"No," Emily said. "It doesn't."

She let it sit.

"What does the stone feel like right now?"

Cameron checked in. "Still there. Heavier."

"What's it doing with 'precious doesn't run a farm'?"

Cameron was quiet for a moment. "Defending it. Like it agrees with me."

Emily waited.

"But something else too." Cameron's brow pulled in slightly. "It's tired."

"Of what?"

"Of running the farm." A pause. "Of proving it can."

Emily nodded once.

"What happens if the stone doesn't have to prove anything?"

Cameron went still.

"So the anger," she said. "It was protecting that?"

"Yes," Emily said. "It was protecting your right to exist."

Cameron exhaled, long and steady.

The fire in Cameron's chest wasn't gone.

But it was no longer burning her from the inside out.

It was warming.

And for the first time, she didn't feel like she had to prove she belonged on her own land.

What do I want?

She was closing the equipment shed when his truck pulled up.

Bruce didn't get out right away. That was something she had noticed about him early on, the way he took a moment before he moved. She used to think it was hesitation. She understood now it was just how he arrived.

She latched the shed and walked toward the truck. He got out as she got close, and they stood in the early dark with the smell of turned earth and the last of the day's heat still in the ground.

"How was it?" he asked.

"Hard." She wasn't used to saying that. She said it anyway.

He nodded. He didn't fill the pause, which was one of the things she trusted about him.

They walked toward the house without deciding to. She pointed out a section of the fence line that needed attention next week, out of habit, because there was always something to point at. He looked at the fence. He didn't say anything about it.

At the porch steps, he stopped. "Can I ask you something?"

"You're going to anyway."

"What do you want?" he said. "Not for the farm. For yourself. If the farm didn't need anything tomorrow."

She opened her mouth.

What came out first was the south pasture. A full sentence about soil amendments and the timing of the cover crop before she caught herself halfway through it and stopped.

He waited.

She looked at the fence line she'd pointed at. She looked at the field beyond it, going dark. She had been working this land since she was eight years old. She knew every corner of it. She was not sure she knew the answer to his question.

"I don't know," she said. She said it like it cost something.

"Okay," he said. That was all.

She looked at him. He wasn't bothered. He wasn't pushing her toward an answer she didn't have. He was just standing there like the question could wait, like he had been waiting already and was prepared to keep waiting.

"Maybe the river," she said. It came out quieter than she intended. "I used to go to the river. Before I was old enough to be useful."

He didn't say anything for a moment. Then: "I know a good spot."

"I know a good spot too," she said.

Something settled. Not resolved. Just set down for a moment.

She went inside. He drove home the long way, which she wouldn't find out until later, and by then it wouldn't surprise her.

CHAPTER 13

Who Are You Becoming

Emily set her folder on the table. They were all already seated when she arrived.

That hadn't happened before.

She didn't comment on it.

"I want to start with the second tool," she said. "When something good happened, did you try to lean into it? Let it be bigger?" She looked around the table. "What did your body do?"

The silence was shorter than it used to be.

"I let someone else present at the county meeting this week." Cameron didn't add what she would have added six months ago, the part about staying close, about reviewing the deck in advance. "It went better than I would have done it."

"What happened in your body?"

Cameron was quiet for a moment. "I tried to lean into it. The way you said." She looked at the table. "The good was there. I could feel it." A pause. "But I couldn't make it bigger. Something was still there, and it was..." She looked for the word. "Like a ceiling."

"What does the ceiling do?"

"Keeps the good from moving all the way through." She said it evenly, like someone reading a gauge. "I didn't know there was a ceiling until I tried to push past it."

Theodore had been listening. "I used the naming tool more than the sitting one," he said. "Every time Evan came up in my head, I named it. The crew is filming." He paused. "I didn't sit with anything good. I don't think I let anything be good long enough."

"That's data," Emily said.

Roman hadn't spoken. Emily looked at him briefly. He picked up his water glass and set it back down.

"I tracked it," he said. "How many times a day the crew showed up." He looked at the table. "Eleven times Tuesday. Fourteen on Thursday." A pause. "I didn't get to the sitting one."

"Why not?"

"I told myself I'd get to it."

Emily held his gaze a moment longer. "Anything else?"

Roman set the glass down. "I went to see the Ellison and Wright founder." A pause. "I know those numbers better than anyone in that room. I decided that wasn't the meeting for them." He looked at the table. "I didn't bring them."

The room was quiet. Not the waiting kind. The absorbing kind.

"How did it go?" Emily asked.

"He wants to meet again." Roman looked at the table. "I've been trying to figure out what I said wrong."

Emily held it a moment.

Then: "Roman, say that again."

He looked up. "He wants to meet again."

"The part before that."

A pause. "I've been trying to figure out what I said wrong."

Nobody moved. Emily didn't explain it. She let the room do the work.

"Do you notice what you just did?" Emily said. "The meeting went well. And your nervous system went looking for the mistake."

She moved to the board.

"We talked in an earlier session about how cycles work. How a loop that doesn't close stays open. The file stays active." She looked around the table. "What I want to add today is what that open file does to your identity. Because this is the part most people miss."

"You can decide you want to be someone different. You can name it, write it down, say it out loud. And the moment something high-stakes happens, the old file activates. Not because you're weak. Because it's still running. And a running file doesn't just drive your behavior. It shapes how you see yourself."

Roman's expression hadn't changed, but something behind it had shifted slightly.

"I've been doing the work," he said. "I've been naming the crew. I know the file is there."

"Knowing it's there is different from closing it."

"I'll get to it."

Emily looked at him. Not unkindly. "You said that about the other tool, too."

The room was quiet.

"I'm not saying this to push you," she said. "I'm saying it because you just told us you went into a meeting differently than you've ever gone into one. No projections. And it went well. And your first move after was to find the flaw." She paused. "The cycle isn't optional maintenance you get to schedule. It's the thing that decides whether the new identity has any room to run."

Roman looked at the table. "So I can't go in without the deck and actually believe it was the right call until the file closes."

"You can try. A lot of people do. But the inner critic is still in the director's chair. It's been there a long time. When something high-stakes happens, it's the one deciding which reel plays. And you already know where it takes you."

Roman's jaw clenched. "I hate how logical this is."

"Does it land?"

A pause. "Yes."

· · ·

Nobody filled the silence quickly. The room understood it needed to sit there.

Emily moved back to the board.

"Has anyone ever thought: when I hit that number, then I'll know I made it? The nicer car. The nicer house. One more credential, one more win, and then I'll know."

Nobody rushed to answer. But nobody looked at the table either.

"When a cycle stays incomplete, the inner critic is still in the room. Still scanning. Still rooted in the negative belief." She looked around the table. "So the goals you set from that place are designed to do one of two things: outrun the belief, or prove it wrong." She paused. "Exhausting fuel. Because the file never closes. You hit the goal and the inner critic is already pointing at the next thing you haven't proved yet."

Cameron exhaled. Not dramatically. Just enough.

"Not a character flaw," Emily said. "When the inner critic is still in the director's chair, the goals it helps you set are designed to keep you safe from the belief. Not to change it. The pattern isn't the problem. The belief fueling it is."

She picked up the marker.

"Which is why the point isn't to stop the pattern through willpower. Most of you know that by now. You've caught the crew. You've named it. You've sat at your stall and looked at your certification and felt the list start before the good feeling finished." She looked at Cameron briefly. "Willpower can interrupt the pattern. It can't change what's fueling it."

"When the cycle closes," Emily said, "you're not outrunning the belief anymore. The inner critic isn't in the chair." She set the marker down. "For the first time, you have a real choice. Not about what to achieve. About who you want to be."

She looked around the table.

"Identity is how you see yourself. The way you talk to yourself about yourself. It shapes what you think is possible before you ever set a goal." She looked at the board. "When you're running from who you saw yourself through the lens of your beliefs, your goals are designed to escape it or disprove it. When you choose a new one, your goals start to look different."

"The simplest way in: finish this sentence." She wrote on the board. "I'm the kind of person who."

She looked at them.

"Not a wish. Not a goal. A declaration about who you already are in the process of becoming. You start small. I'm the kind of person who finishes what they start. I'm the kind of person who shows up. I'm the kind of person who trusts their read." She paused. "Your brain wants to be right. When you plant the identity, it starts looking for evidence. And it finds it." She paused. "In the positive crew's footage."

She moved back to the board and drew two columns. Left: Proving Goal. Right: Identity Goal.

"A proving goal is built to answer the inner critic. To make it stop, or prove it wrong. There's nothing wrong with the goal itself. The goals you've set from that place are real. They produced real results." She looked around. "The problem is what they cost. You can't let the achievement land. You can't rest on what you built. The inner critic doesn't let it count. It just updates the requirement. And the energy you're spending trying to satisfy it never comes back." She paused. "So what happens when you hit the goal?"

"You just set the next one," Cameron said.

"Because you still don't feel safe. The achievement goes in the positive crew's footage. But the inner critic is still in the chair, still scanning, and it doesn't register the way it should. Still asking: is that enough? Does that count? What do you have to do to make it permanent?"

The room was quiet.

"An identity goal is different. It starts with the question: given who I've decided to be, what do I build next? Not what do I need to prove. What does this person do from here?"

She gave them a moment.

"Take the thing you most want to build in the next year. Don't overthink it." She paused. "Proving goal or identity goal?"

Cameron's jaw tightened the way it did when something landed before she was ready. "Mine is a proving goal."

"Most first drafts are," Emily said. Not failure."

"What do I do with it?"

"You don't throw it away. You look at the reason underneath it." Emily looked at her steadily. "Same farm. Same regenerative work. Same ambition. But instead of: I'm going to make this undeniable so no one can question my right to be here." She paused. "What if it became: I'm building something I believe in, because that's who I am."

Cameron was quiet for a long moment. "That's the same goal."

"Is it?"

Longer quiet.

"No," Cameron said. "It doesn't feel the same at all."

Theodore turned his watch once around his wrist. "I've been framing the Evan pitch as: does marketing help the shop survive. But that's a proving goal. The shop needs to survive because otherwise the work doesn't count." He looked at the table. "What if I just decide the work deserves to be seen. And I'm the one who decides that."

Emily was quiet for a moment. "What changes if you decide that?"

"I'd call Evan back," Theodore said. "And actually listen."

Emily nodded once. She looked at Roman.

He hadn't moved. But something had settled in him, the way things do when a person has stopped arguing with a fact and started living with it instead.

"The Ellison and Wright deal," Emily said. "Proving goal or identity goal?"

Roman considered it. "Both."

"Say more."

"There's a version where I'm proving the read was right." He looked at the table. "And there's a version where it's just the next right thing. And I'm the person who builds the next right thing."

"Which one was in the room when you were running the second pass on the projections?"

A pause. Not long.

"The first one."

"What do the projections tell you?" Emily asked.

Roman considered. "Whether the numbers support the decision."

"And when they don't?"

"I find better numbers."

"What are you waiting for them to confirm?"

The room was quiet. Roman's answer took longer than his others.

"That I'm not wrong."

"Are you usually wrong?"

"No."

"So what's the second pass for?"

His jaw set. Not the answer he wanted. "Due diligence."

"Is it?"

He looked at her. The look was not warm. "Yes."

Emily waited.

Roman set his pen down. Not carefully. "I've spent eleven years building a track record. Running the numbers isn't doubt. It's rigor."

"What would happen if you skipped them?"

"Nothing would happen. That's not the point."

"What is the point?"

He looked at her. The look said he didn't appreciate the question. "Doing it right."

"What does doing it right protect?"

A longer silence.

Roman picked up his pen. Put it back down. "I heard you earlier. The file." He looked at the table. "I know what you're saying."

"What am I saying?"

"That I don't trust myself." He said it as if he were objecting to a charge. "That every extra pass I run is the file looking for permission it doesn't need."

"Is that what I said?"

His jaw shifted. "It's what you meant."

Emily waited.

"It's accurate," he said finally. Not happily. "I hate that it's accurate."

Nobody filled the silence quickly. Not the waiting kind. The staying kind.

"I want to give you one more tool," she said. "It's deceptively simple." She looked around the table. "Every morning, one question: What would the person I'm becoming do today?"

She let it sit.

"Not the person you were at eleven. Not the person who built their survival strategy around a belief planted before they could question it. The person you are actively deciding to become." She paused. "You don't have to answer the question perfectly. You just have to ask it. Because the asking shifts the operating system."

Jade had been writing. She looked up. "What if the answer isn't clear yet?"

"Then staying curious about the question is the work. That's enough." Emily looked at her. "You don't have to know who you're becoming to start becoming them. You just have to take one action the wound wouldn't have taken."

Jade looked back down at her sketchbook. She was drawing something small in the margin. Not a piece. Just a mark.

"One more thing before we close," Emily said.

"You are going to have setbacks. Weeks where the negative crew runs a lot of footage. Where the old behavior shows up, and the wound goal takes over, and you can't remember who you were becoming." She paused. "That is not failure. That's the nervous system doing what it knows."

"Even when you close the loops. Even when you step out of the director's chair and make a different decision about who you are and what you're building." She paused. "The old behavior is going to feel safe. You've been running those same grooves for decades. The brain doesn't care that you've made a new decision. It's going to offer you the familiar road every single time."

She drew a line on the board. Five marks on it.

"There are five stages to behavior change. The first: you do the thing and don't even notice. The inner critic is driving, and you don't know it. The second: you notice hours later. You're in bed, and you realize what happened. The third: you notice sooner. Not always in time to apologize. But earlier than before. The fourth: you notice in the moment. The pattern is still running. But you see it. The fifth: you feel it coming before it happens. And you choose differently."

She looked around the table.

"Every stage is progress. The eight-hour-later version is not the same as not noticing at all. Don't discount it." She paused. "And you don't get to stage five through determination. You get there by completing the cycles, so the old behavior runs out of fuel. The belief underneath it changes. And then the groove stops feeling like the safe road."

"The question isn't whether you return to the old pattern. It's how long you stay there before you notice. And whether noticing has gotten faster." She looked around the table. "It will get faster. That's what this work does."

She picked up her folder.

"Who are you becoming? Ask it every morning. Let the answer change as you change." She paused at the edge of the table. "And trust that the person showing up to ask the question is already someone different from who walked into this room the first week."

They left in ones and twos. The room settled back into itself.

Roman was the last one out. He paused in the doorway, not looking back so much as looking forward.

CHAPTER 14

Roman, The Calculation He Can't Run

The screen connected at exactly nine o'clock. Emily was already on.

"Roman," she said.

"Morning." He had taken the call in his office. The city was visible through the window behind him.

"How are you after last week?"

"Different than I expected." He reached for his water. "I've been running the session back. The projections piece. I keep arriving at the same answer, and I don't particularly like it."

"What's the answer?"

"That I've been running them from a place of proving, not identity. Even the name of them bugs me."

"You tracked the inner critic this week."

"Eleven times Tuesday. Fourteen on Thursday. Every time I went back to the numbers. Every time I delayed a decision I already knew the answer to." He set the water down. "I didn't get to the sitting tool."

"How did things go with Ellison this week?"

"He wants to move forward. I put together a proposal. Owner financing, so the terms stay between us and not a bank." He looked at the folder on the desk beside him. "I haven't sent it. I ran the numbers a third time last night."

Emily looked at him. "I think you know where we're going today."

Roman's jaw shifted slightly. "Yes."

Emily pulled up the shared screen. He recognized it from their first session. His scores, side by side.

"Growth area: acquiring and integrating a firm to double your current size. I trust myself. You scored it a four."

Roman looked at the number. "Yes."

"Strength area: reviewing structural plans, solving technical architectural problems. I trust myself. An eight."

"Yes."

"Same person. Four points apart, depending on which room you're standing in."

"The technical trust I've built," he said. "There's a right answer, and I know how to find it. The acquisition has no blueprint."

"You've reviewed the numbers three times," she said. "You know them better than anyone in that room. The projections are strong. The founder trusts you." She paused. "What's in the way?"

"That's the question I keep asking myself."

"What do you get back?"

"Something I can't calculate."

"Let's go find it." She paused. "Close your eyes if you're willing. I want you to think about sending that proposal. Not the analysis. Just the act of sending it. Notice what happens in your body."

Roman adjusted his position slightly. He closed his eyes.

The silence ran for several seconds.

"There's something in my chest," he said finally.

"Good. Stay with it. Don't try to explain it yet. Just notice it."

He was quiet.

"Can you find the edges of it? Where does it start and where does it stop?"

Roman frowned slightly, the way he frowned at a load calculation that didn't resolve cleanly. "It's across the whole chest. But it's stronger in the middle."

"Is there a shape to it?"

"A band." He said it like he was reading a blueprint. "Wide. Across the sternum."

"Temperature?"

"Warm. Not hot. Just warm."

"Color?"

A pause. "Red."

"Okay." Emily's voice was easy. "I want you to zoom in on it. Like you're studying a detail in a set of plans. Look at it from every angle. When you do that, does it change in any way?"

Roman concentrated. "It gets tighter when I look directly at it."

"Good. I want you to relax into it. Like you're settling into a chair at the end of a long day. No problem. There's just a warm red band across your chest. It's not going to hurt you. Can you let it be there?"

A longer silence.

"It's not loosening," he said.

"That's okay. Just keep settling."

Several seconds passed.

"It's a little less aggressive," he said. "Like it stopped pressing harder."

"Good. Now this next part, you always love it." Emily kept her voice steady.

Roman opened his eyes briefly, then closed them again. "I still think it's dumb to express gratitude for a sensation making it hard to breathe."

"I know."

He was quiet for a moment. Then: "All right. Thank you for whatever you're doing."

"What happens when you do that?"

"It loosens. Slightly." He sounded like a man reporting data he didn't expect. "That's strange."

"It has a message for you. That's what we are here for." Emily's voice was gentle but direct. "I want you to imagine handing it a microphone. Turn the volume up if you need to. Ask it: what have you been trying to tell me? And just notice what comes up. It might be a word. It might be a memory. Could be a movie. Don't edit it."

The silence was longer this time.

Roman's expression shifted. His face did something it hadn't done for most of the call.

"You are not your dad."

He said it quietly. Like he wasn't sure if he was reporting it or saying it.

"Stay with that," Emily said. "When you think, 'I am not my dad.' What else comes up? Is there any story that jumps out?"

He opened his eyes. He looked at something past the camera for a moment, then back. "My father answered technical questions. He never explained the reasoning behind his final calls. I watched him make decisions my entire life without knowing how he made them." He paused. "I assumed certainty was the requirement. That if you doubted, you didn't show it. That's what leadership looked like."

"And when he died?" Emily asked.

"There was no walkthrough. No gradual handoff." Roman's voice stayed even. Controlled. "One day I'm at a funeral, and then it was just mine. Forty-two people looking to me for direction." He was quiet for a moment. "And somewhere in the weeks after that, I decided something."

Emily waited.

"That if he believed I was ready, he would have prepared me. Since he never bothered to hand over the reins or even train me, he must not have trusted me."

Neither of them spoke.

"That belief has been running the second pass every time," Emily said. "Every projection. Every extra review. Every decision you already knew the answer to."

"Yes."

Emily leaned slightly forward. "Roman. You stabilized the firm. You made it more profitable than your father left it. And the man who built Ellison and Wright over thirty years, who had every option available to him, looked at everything and chose you." She paused. "Not because of your projections. Because of your read."

Roman looked at the table.

"Your father's certainty wasn't the same as being right," Emily said. "It was just his way. You've been trying to inherit his style instead of building your own."

The room was quiet for a long moment.

"Notice what's happening in your chest right now," she said.

Roman checked in. "The band is still there. But it's different. Looser." He paused. "More like a reminder than a restraint."

"Good. It's beginning to update." She kept her voice warm. "I want you to say something out loud. Don't perform it. Just say it and notice what your body does." She paused. "I trust myself."

Roman took a breath. "I trust myself."

He was quiet.

"It doesn't feel completely true," he said.

"Sometimes it doesn't. Especially with something that's been running this long. "Emily's voice was straightforward. "You say it. You say it again. You send the proposal. And every time you catch the inner critic back in the director's chair, you name it, and you make a different call. That's what moves the number."

"Before we close, I want to give you two things to work with." Emily leaned back slightly. "Daily: say 'I trust myself' out loud.

Once. Morning is good if that works for you. Don't wait for it to feel true. Just say it and notice where it lands in your body. That's the only job. Notice, and bring the information back."

Roman nodded.

"And specifically," she said, "the next time you feel the pull to run the numbers again, I want you to pause. Just for a moment. Name whose voice is sending you back. Not to blame anyone. Just as information. Is it your read? Or is it the inner critic asking for one more confirmation it doesn't actually need?"

"I'll know the difference?" Roman asked.

"You will," she said. "That's why this is the homework."

She looked at him for a moment. "Send the proposal, Roman."

Something in his expression shifted. Not a smile. More like a door opening a crack.

"I'll let you know how he responds," he said.

* * *

Stacked in the Corner

He drove past his exit twice, just letting the city move around him. Not thinking, exactly. For the first time all week, he wasn't running the numbers.

When he finally pulled into the garage, he sat in the car for a moment.

The tarp was against the back wall, the way it had been for two and a half years.

He got out of the car.

He pulled the cover off in one motion, the way his father used to, without ceremony. The bike was a 1974 Triumph Bonneville. His father had bought it at twenty-six and kept it the way other men kept promises.

He crouched. The chrome needed work. He'd known that before he covered it.

He got it started on the third try.

Roman ran his hand along the tank. The chrome was dusty but clean underneath.

He did not think about the session. He did not think about the proposal sitting in his outbox. He thought about the way the engine used to sound in the early morning, before anyone else was awake, when his father would take it out on the empty streets, and Roman would lie in bed and listen to it go.

He checked the fluids. He checked the battery. He did the things his father had shown him, in the order his father had shown him.

Then he sat on it.

He did not turn the key.

He just sat. For awhile.

When he started, he didn't plan where he was going.

He just rode. His father had tried to explain it once. That you ride until you stop thinking in straight lines. Roman hadn't understood it then.

Theodore's shop sat off the main road on a property that had more trees than it needed.

Roman pulled in. Cut the engine. Sat for a moment.

Through the workshop window, a light was on.

• • •

Theodore heard him pull up and looked out.

He watched Roman get off the bike and stand next to it. Not looking at the shop, not looking at anything in particular. Just standing the way you stand when you've arrived somewhere and you're still deciding what you came for.

Theodore went back to what he was working on.

Roman came in. He looked around the shop the way he always looked at a new room, reading it, not scanning it. He came around the table and looked at what was open in front of Theodore. A heavy wooden frame was clamped to the bench, its joints exposed. Nearby rested the painting it belonged to, in some stage of cleaning, the varnish on one half still yellowed, the other half already showing what was underneath. A river. Light.

Roman found the low stool in the corner, and he watched Theodore work, the way you watched someone who knew what they were doing.

Theodore didn't ask. He reached for a clamp, then handed it to Roman instead.

Roman held it. Passed it back when it was needed. They worked like that for a while, in the easy rhythm of two people who had grown up handing things to someone without being told to.

"I had my session today," Roman said, eventually.

Theodore didn't look up from what he was doing. "You look like it."

Roman looked at the bench. "Is that good?"

"Means it did something."

They didn't talk for a while after that.

"My father and I never talked," Roman said. "We just worked."

Theodore looked at what was in front of him. "Same."

"I used to think that was enough." Roman turned a piece of scrap molding over in his hands. "That it was actually better. Cleaner."

"I thought that too." Theodore made a small adjustment to the frame's corner. "I'm not sure anymore."

Roman set the molding down. "My son, Andrew, started rehearsals this week."

Theodore glanced at him.

"I went to the first one." Roman looked at the workbench. "Sat in the back so he wouldn't see me and make a thing of it." He was quiet for a moment. "He didn't see me. I don't think. He was up on the stage reading something, and he looked like a different person. Or maybe the same person. I don't know." He paused. "I didn't know he had it in him."

Theodore was quiet for a moment. He set down what he was holding.

"I have a son," he said. "He designs things. Websites, mostly. He sent me a mockup, something he'd built, a way to show the work online." He picked up the chisel again. "I didn't look at it. Not really. For about six months."

Roman waited.

"I looked at it last week." Theodore turned the chisel once in his hand. "It was good. I asked him about the photographs."

"What did he say?"

"He had a lot to say." Theodore almost smiled. "I didn't know that about him either."

The shop was quiet. Somewhere outside, the wind moved through the trees.

"He looked like me," Theodore said. "The way he talked about it." He paused. "I hadn't seen that before."

He didn't say anything else. He picked up where he'd left off.

Roman handed him the mallet without being asked.

They worked until the light changed.

When Roman stood to go, he looked at the bench the way you look at something you helped build, checking that it was sound.

"The bike was his," he said. He wasn't explaining. Just saying it out loud.

Theodore looked at it through the window. "I wondered."

Roman pulled on his jacket. He stood at the door for a moment.

"Thank you," he said.

Theodore nodded once. The same nod as before, in the session room. But here it meant something slightly different.

Here it meant: *I know. Me too.*

• • •

Theodore came in through the kitchen.

Marianne was at the counter with her back to him. She heard him before she turned, the particular sound of his step when he'd been in the shop for hours, slower and more deliberate, the way he moved when his hands had been working something small.

"Dinner's been cold for a while," she said. Not a complaint. Just accounting.

"I know." He set his jacket over the chair. "I'm sorry."

She turned then. She looked at him the way she'd learned to look at him over many years of his silences, reading the thing underneath.

"Roman Hale came by the shop."

She waited.

"We talked for a while."

She didn't say anything right away. Theodore didn't fill the quiet, which wasn't unusual. What was unusual was the way he'd said it. *We talked.* Not *he stopped by.* Not *he needed something.*

"He lost his father three years ago," Theodore said. "No warning. One day, he's there. The next day, he's not. And the firm is Roman's."

"He's trying to do it differently with his son. He doesn't know if he's doing it right." Theodore looked at the table. "He said that out loud."

Marianne was still.

"I told him about Evan. The website mockup." He sat down. "I told him I'd let it sit for six months because I was afraid it would be better than I expected, and I didn't know what to do with that."

She looked at him.

"I haven't said that to anyone," he said.

She was quiet for a long moment. In the distance, she could hear the cicadas, the soundtrack of their evenings.

"No," she said. "You haven't."

She turned back to the counter to fix his plate. He sat at the table and didn't move to help, which meant he was still somewhere inside it.

She set the plate in front of him and sat across from him.

She had been married to his silences for a long time. She knew how to read them. Which ones were simply where he lived, and which ones meant he was still working something through.

This one was the second kind.

She didn't push. Outside, the last of the light went.

CHAPTER 15

What You Hear When It's Quiet

The rain started before anyone arrived.

Emily had set the conference room the same way she always did. Water glasses at each place around the long oak table. The whiteboard wiped clean. The window cracked for air. The sound of rain on the glass was the first thing each of them heard when they came through the door, and something in it seemed to set them at a slower pace.

They were on time, which by now meant they arrived early. Jade and Cameron came in from the lobby, shaking out umbrellas. Julia held the glass door for Theodore. Roman was already inside, standing near the head of the table, watching the rain move across the street below.

They took their seats. Notebooks opened.

Emily let a moment pass before she said anything. She looked around the table, taking in the posture of the room. Roman was sitting further back in his chair than usual. Theodore's hands were resting open on his notebook.

"Last session, I gave you a question to ask every morning: 'Who are you becoming?'" She let her eyes move across them. "I want to go around the table."

Julia said, "The new bookkeeper called with questions twice this week." She looked at her mug. "Both times my first thought was that I'd made a mistake somewhere." She paused. "I hadn't. She just had questions. And I noticed I didn't spend the rest of the day convinced I had."

Cameron filed it simply. "I let one of my field managers make a call without me. It wasn't perfect." She paused. "It was fine."

Jade turned her ring once. "I walked past the Fashion Week application twice this week. Didn't open it, didn't close it." She looked at the table. "I'm calling that progress."

A few of them laughed. Light, brief. It cleared something.

Emily looked at Theodore.

He looked at the table before he spoke. Not to avoid it. Just the way he moved through things.

"I told Marianne why I'd let Evan's mockup sit." He paused. "The real reason. I was afraid it would be better than I expected. And I didn't know what to do with that."

"What happened when you told her?" Emily asked.

Theodore's thumb moved to the edge of his watchband. "She sat with me." He stopped. "We've been married thirty-one years. I've never said anything like that to her."

He looked up, briefly. "I didn't know that was possible."

Emily held it for a moment. Then she looked at Roman.

Roman brought his eyes back from the window. "I went to Andrew's rehearsal. Sat in the back. He didn't see me." He paused. "He forgot a line. Just stopped. Then he found it and kept going."

"Nobody cared," he said. "The other kids didn't stop. The director didn't stop. The whole room kept moving." He was quiet for a moment, looking at his hands. "I've been treating uncertainty like it disqualifies you. For thirty years. I've been passing that on without knowing it."

The room was very still.

"What does it feel like to see that?" Emily asked.

Roman looked up. The analytical cadence was gone from his voice. "Like running an equation and realizing the value I entered thirty years ago was wrong. Every answer I got from it." He stopped. "Was wrong."

Emily held the room.

"Yeah," she said.

She looked at the table for a moment.

"This is what happens when the work starts landing. You see clearly, sometimes for the first time, what you built to stay safe. How long it has been running. What it cost you." She paused. "And sometimes the first thing that comes up isn't relief."

Cameron's jaw was tight. She was looking at the wood grain on the table.

"That's where I want to start today."

"I want to talk about forgiveness," Emily said.

She let that sit before she continued.

"Not the kind you think you've done already. Not the decision you made once and filed away." She looked around the table. "When someone hurts you, you can sometimes get to a place, with enough time or enough work, where you can look at what they did and say: okay. I see how they got there. They were doing the best they could. The skills they had. The culture they were raised in. Their own pain." She paused. "You can see it wasn't malicious. Just limited."

Cameron said, "I can see that with my dad." She wasn't looking up. "He wanted a son. I was the one who stayed and ran it." She paused. "His disappointment was there before I touched anything. Before the first decision I made. I thought for a long time if I just got the yields right, that would be enough. But I was trying to fix something that wasn't actually about the yields."

She looked at the grain of the table. "He did the best he could with what he was given. That's probably true." She stopped. "It still took me a long time to stop trying to be someone he could be proud of."

Emily let that sit.

"Did it feel finished?" she asked. "When you got there?"

Cameron was quiet.

"This is what I want to slow down on." Emily walked a few steps and stopped. "Because forgiveness isn't always a single event. Sometimes someone hurts you, and the damage keeps showing up. Long after you've forgiven them. Long after you think you're past it."

She looked at the table.

"Think about it this way. Someone cuts off your foot. You forgive them. You mean it. You make peace with it." She paused. "But five years later, you fall down. You would have caught yourself if your foot was still there. And the grief comes back. The anger comes back."

Nobody moved.

"You have to forgive them again," Emily said. "Not because you did it wrong the first time. Because your life is different as a consequence of what they did. Every time that shows up, you may have to forgive them again for the way your life will keep being different."

Julia was very still.

"Most people think that means the original forgiveness didn't take," Emily said. "It did. You just didn't know yet all the places it would keep mattering."

Theodore said, quietly, "You think you've settled it. Then it turns up somewhere you didn't expect."

"Yes," Emily said. "Exactly that."

She turned back toward the table.

"Now." She looked around the room. "What happens when you turn that same process toward yourself?"

"You can usually reason your way to understanding someone else," Emily said. "See the limits they were working from. But when the choices were yours, and the damage was yours, and you're the one who has to forgive yourself for it." She stopped. "That's harder."

Julia looked down at her hands.

"And then there's the layer underneath that," Emily said. "You also have to forgive yourself for how you treated yourself after. All the ways you pushed through, or shut down, or told yourself to be better without asking if you were okay."

Jade turned her ring once around her finger.

"All of this leads to self-judgment. And the inner critic loves self-judgment. It's its best tool." Emily paused. "So if we want to loosen the inner critic's grip, what we need to develop is self-compassion."

"How?" Theodore asked. The precision in his voice was still there, but it was softer.

"Self-compassion starts with noticing your pain," Emily said. "It requires you to stop turning a blind eye to the discomfort you're carrying. Stop telling yourself to suck it up."

She walked back toward the whiteboard.

"Once you've noticed it, you have to let yourself be moved by it. Not perform it. Not push it aside. Just let it matter." She paused. "And then you have to understand that pain, failure, and rejection are not evidence that something is wrong with you. They're part of being human. The inner critic tells you that every hard thing is a catastrophe. Self-compassion says: This is hard. That's allowed."

"This requires curiosity," Emily added. "And if your nervous system doesn't feel safe, it won't let you be curious. If a lion is chasing you, you don't stop to look at flowers." She turned to them. "So you have to calm the system first. And then you meet yourself with questions instead of verdicts. Am I tired? Am I hungry? Am I overwhelmed? What do I need right now to feel safe?"

She let the questions hang in the room.

"When you start asking those questions," Emily said, "you realize your mind isn't a single, unified voice. It's a committee.

And usually, the loudest voices are the only ones we let speak. The critic. The protector. The driver."

She turned to the board and wrote two numbers, leaving a wide space between them.

8   80

"If you want to understand the armor you built, and what it looks like to put it down," she said, turning back to the table, "I want to introduce you to two committee members most people haven't fully consulted."

She pointed to the 8.

"Think about yourself at eight years old. Seven, eight, nine. Somewhere in that window. The version that existed before most of the big stories about you got written. Before you learned to make yourself smaller, or harder, or more useful, or more invisible. Before you knew what the rules were."

She paused.

"Let that version come to mind. Not the current version. Not the future one you're building toward. The one present when you first learned something about whether you were enough, whether you were safe to be fully seen, whether you deserved the space you were in."

She let her voice slow.

"Don't go looking. Just let them come."

The rain.

Cameron was in a field. She didn't choose it. It was just where she went.

The girl was small. Rubber boots a size too big, moving fast the way children move when they've learned that usefulness is a language adults can hear. Her father was ahead of her. Not far. She could feel the distance and was working to close it.

The girl didn't look up to see if he was watching. She already knew the answer to that.

Cameron watched her carry something. A bucket, a bag of feed, something heavier than it should have been. She watched the girl set it down and turn back for more. She stopped once, just for a second, standing still in the field. Her father didn't turn around. She picked up the next thing and kept going.

She wanted to say something to her. She didn't know what.

Jade found the dresser before she found the girl.

The velvet box. The weight of it in small hands. The stone caught the afternoon light from a window that let in too much of it.

She remembered what it felt like to turn that ring and understand something had changed. Love could be something you took off. It could live in a box at the back of a drawer.

The girl holding it was eight. She wasn't crying. She was paying very close attention.

Julia was in her mother's kitchen.

She was small enough that the counter was still at eye level. Her mother was somewhere behind her, moving between the stove and the sink. Saturday morning. The radio low.

Julia had her hands in bread dough. Her mother had started it and let her finish. She didn't know how she knew what to do with it. She just did.

The kitchen smelled like butter and something baking, and whatever her mother wore on weekends. Julia wasn't thinking about anything. She was just there, her hands knowing things her brain hadn't caught up to yet.

Theodore found himself in the workshop.

His father's lamp in the corner, casting the same circle of light over the workbench it always had. His father's hands moving over a piece of damaged walnut, feeling for something Theodore couldn't see yet, wasn't old enough yet to see. Not explaining. Just working and letting the boy stand close.

Theodore was maybe eleven. He stood near enough to watch.

The work didn't have to be seen to matter. It just had to be. He had known that once, the way you know the smell of a room you grew up in. Without thinking about it. Without defending it. Just true. It didn't have to be better than expected. It just had to be.

Roman was at a job site.

The hard hat was too big. He'd pushed it back so he could see properly. His father was talking to a contractor about a load-bearing change, something about the original plans not accounting for the addition. His father made a call. Clean. Final. The contractor nodded and walked away.

Roman had asked, "How did you know?"

His father looked at him and answered a different question. Gave him the structural reasoning. The numbers. The code requirements. All of it accurate. None of it what the boy had asked.

What the boy had actually asked was. What does it feel like from the inside when you don't know, and you decide anyway?

He hadn't known how to say that. So he took his father's answer and made it a rule. That you were supposed to "just know." Certainty was the entry requirement. Doubt meant you weren't ready.

He'd been carrying that for thirty years. Right up until he sat in the back of an auditorium, watched his son grow uncertain, and realized it was beautiful.

"Take a breath," Emily said. "And come back."

She gave them a full moment.

"What does that version of you need to know?"

The question was not complicated. It was also not easy.

Cameron opened her eyes. She looked at the table first, then at Emily. "She needs to know she already belongs there. Before she hauled anything. Before she proved anything."

Emily nodded. "If she walked into this room right now, carrying something too heavy for her. Would you tell her to suck it up?"

Cameron's jaw tightened. "No."

"No," Emily agreed. "You would say: that looks heavy. You would say: " You don't have to carry that anymore." She looked around the table. "Why is it so much harder to say that to yourself?"

Jade had her small notebook open. She was writing something, pressing down on the pen. Not for the room. Just so she wouldn't lose it.

Julia said, "She needs to know it was always her." She stopped. "Not just the kitchen part. The whole thing."

Theodore was quiet for a long time. When he spoke, it was carefully, the way he was careful with things that required precision. "He needs to know the work was real. It always was. The world getting louder doesn't change what the work is."

Roman was last. He hadn't moved since he came back. When he spoke, it was low.

"He needed someone to tell him it was okay not to know yet. Uncertainty didn't mean disqualified." He looked up. "I was ten. I didn't know enough to say that to him. But I think I can say it now."

The room held it.

Emily let the silence sit before she added anything.

"Here's what I find," she said. "Those versions of you are still there. They didn't go anywhere. And when we don't acknowledge them, they find the driver's seat. They make decisions from places we don't notice."

She looked around the table.

"But they don't have to drive. They can ride along. They can be in the car. You can let them be glad they're with you. The eight-year-old who would be floored by your life. The one needing to know you're glad she made it this far."

She stopped.

"Are you glad they're there?"

It was not rhetorical.

Cameron said, "I've been trying to outrun her since I was old enough to drive a tractor."

Jade looked at her. "I know."

Those two sentences held more than most conversations. Emily didn't add to them.

Julia said, after a while, "What do we do with that? Practically."

"You start by stopping," Emily said. "Every time you catch yourself abandoning one of those parts. Dismissing the fear, overriding the doubt without listening to it, pushing through without asking what it needs. You pause. You say: I hear you. You're allowed to be here. You can't drive, but you can ride."

"That sounds simple," Cameron said.

"It sounds simple," Emily agreed. "It takes years."

Theodore said, "What do they need? Specifically."

"Usually?" Emily said. "A plan. Reassurance that if things go wrong, the failure won't be catastrophic. Evidence they were right about something, at some point." She tilted her head. "And sometimes they just need to hear: I'm glad you're with me. You got us here. You don't have to be scared anymore."

Roman was looking at his hands again.

"The part of you doubting," Emily continued, "is not your enemy. It's one of the oldest parts of you. It developed when you were trying to survive something. The work is not to silence it. It's to let it know the situation has changed."

Emily turned back to the whiteboard. She tapped the marker against the second number. The 80.

"And now the eighty-year-old." Emily turned to the other side of the board. "The one who is still kicking at eighty. Still sharp. Still in the room. This version of you has already lived through the thing you fear most, and some version of you survived it."

She looked around the table.

"What does that version of you say about the thing you've been holding so tightly?"

Julia said, almost to herself. "She says stop overthinking it."

"Probably," Emily said. "Yes."

Cameron didn't look up. "She says, put it down. You're tired."

Jade looked at the table. "She says stop making people prove it."

Theodore said, after a moment, "He says I waited too long to talk to her."

Roman was last. His voice was low. "He says go to the rehearsals."

The room was quiet.

At the end of the session, Emily asked them to write down one thing.

Not a goal. Not an action step.

One thing the younger version of themselves needed to hear. Something she suspected they still needed to hear for themselves.

"You don't have to share it," she said. "You don't have to do anything with it today. Just put it in your toolkit so you don't lose it before you get to your car."

The room was filled with the sound of pens.

When they were gathering their things, Roman lingered. Emily was at the whiteboard, erasing the two numbers. He stood near the door but didn't move through it.

"I have a question," he said.

She turned.

"My son, Andrew." He paused. "The eight-year-old version of him." Another pause, shorter. "What would he need to hear?"

Emily looked at him. "What do you think he'd need?"

Roman looked at the window. Outside, the rain had slowed to something lighter, almost nothing.

"I'm glad he's who he is," he said. "Not who I assumed he'd want to be."

He picked up his bag. He didn't wait for her to respond, and she didn't try to catch him. Some things don't need a response. They just need to be said out loud once, in a room where someone hears them, before you take them home and start the longer work.

The door closed.

Emily turned back to the whiteboard. She left it blank.

• • •

The last customer left at six. The kitchen staff cleared out by seven-thirty. Julia locked the front door, turned the sign, and went back to finish what she'd started.

The back office at the original location was barely a room. A desk, two chairs, a filing cabinet with a drawer that stuck. The second chair had been there so long she had stopped seeing it.

She opened the laptop. The spreadsheet Marcus had built for vendor reconciliation was the third tab, same as always. She'd used it every month for a year, working through the rows the way he set them up, following his logic even when it moved differently than her own.

She got about halfway through before she noticed.

She had restructured the produce column. She didn't know when. Sometime in the last few months, she had quietly reorganized the way the rows worked. Shifted the seasonal vendors to a separate section, added a column he hadn't thought to include, changed the formula in a way that caught something his version didn't. She sat back and looked at it.

It was better. Not dramatically. Just more like the way she thought.

She looked at it for a long moment.

The kitchen was quiet. The smell of the day was still in the air. Bread and coffee and the faint sweet edge of the cinnamon rolls she pulled at four that morning. She'd been doing that since Henri. Long before Marcus. Long before the second location. Long before any of it.

She closed the laptop.

The second chair was across from her, the way it always was. She looked at it. She didn't move it. She wasn't ready to name what moving it would mean.

But she got up and went back to the kitchen, which was hers. Which had always been hers.

She turned off the light in the back office and left the spreadsheet open, the cursor blinking in a column she built herself without meaning to.

The kitchen window faced the street. She stood at the counter for a moment, looking out at the space next door. Dark now. Had been for a few months.

She looked at it longer than she usually did.

Then she went back to work.

CHAPTER 16

Jade,
The Invisible Join

Her last customer of the afternoon had come in for a repair and stayed forty minutes. That was usually how it went. Jade would ask one question about the piece and then another, and by the time she looked up, she knew about the grandmother who wore it, the daughter who would inherit it, and the reason it had been in a drawer for three years. She said goodbye twice and meant it both times.

She had four minutes before the call.

• • •

Emily was already on when Jade connected, slightly breathless. Behind her, the workbench was mid-project. Gemstones caught the afternoon light. Half-finished sketches covered the wall above them. She touched her ring without seeming to notice she was doing it.

"Hi. Sorry, a customer stayed longer than I expected."

"Don't apologize," Emily said. "Take a breath."

Jade laughed, a little surprised. She breathed. "Okay. Better."

"You're still in the shop."

"I do everything here." She glanced back briefly. "It's mine."

Emily studied her for a moment. "What does it feel like when you're in there working?"

"Safe," Jade said. "Like I know exactly what I'm doing."

"And outside of it?"

She glanced toward the workbench. "Less sure."

Emily nodded once. "Let's start there."

She glanced at her notes, then back at the screen. "Your boutique scores are strong. Designing meaningful pieces. Connecting deeply with customers. Trusting your instincts in the work. That's not performance. That's real." She paused. "On the other side: 'I am lovable' when it comes to stepping into a bigger stage. Being seen in a competitive room. Letting the work be judged by strangers." She looked up. "A two."

Jade looked at the screen for a moment. "Two sounds about right."

"Six points apart," Emily said. "Same person. Same week."

Jade didn't say anything.

"I want to come back to Fashion Week today."

"Okay."

"Where are you with it?"

"Still sitting on it." She turned the ring. "The boutique show keeps feeling like the right call. Practical. Smart. One is enough."

"Is that what you actually think?"

Jade looked at her hands. "No," she said. "I think I'm scared of the room."

"Say more about that."

"It's full of people who've been doing this longer than me. Designers with press. With followings. They'll walk past my table and either stop or they won't, and there's no relationship, no context. Just the work sitting there, and them deciding."

"And the boutique show feels different because..." Emily said.

"The shop owners have already self-selected. They're there to find someone. It feels more like being chosen than being evaluated."

Emily held that for a moment.

"What's the difference, in your body, between those two?"

Jade tilted her head slightly, going inward. "Fashion Week feels like standing in a hallway waiting to see if anyone knocks."

"And the boutique show?"

"Like someone already rang the bell."

"So at Fashion Week," Emily said, "no one's already decided they want you."

Jade was quiet. "Yeah," she said.

Emily let the silence sit. She didn't rush to the next question.

"Here's what I want to explore with you today," Emily said. "Not which one is the better business decision. That's not the real question. The real question is what it would mean if you showed everything you had and the stylists moved on."

"That's not a business question," Jade said.

"No," Emily said. "It's not."

Jade's shoulders lifted slightly. Her ring went still.

"Okay," Emily said. "Close your eyes. Picture yourself at Fashion Week. You've set up your display. The pieces are out. The light is hitting the stones the way you imagined. And then a stylist walks past. Doesn't stop. Doesn't look back."

Jade closed her eyes.

"What happens in your body?"

"My chest. And my neck. Like a tightness."

"Don't try to get rid of it. Let's zoom in on it." Emily's voice was steady. "Find the edges of that sensation. Walk all around it. Where does it start and where does it stop?"

Jade was quiet for a moment. "It's across my chest. Both sides. Like something pressing flat against me."

"Does it have a shape?"

Jade tilted her head slightly, still with her eyes closed. "Oval. Like a bag of sand. Just sitting there."

"Is there a color that goes with it?"

"Gray. Heavy gray."

"Any texture? Smooth, rough, something else?"

"Dense. Like wet clay."

"Does it have a temperature?"

"Cold."

"Good," Emily said. "Now I want you to relax into it. Not push it away, not fix it. Just like you'd ease into a hot tub. It's just a sensation. It's not going to hurt you. When you relax into it, does it get bigger, smaller, or stay the same?"

Jade breathed slowly. "It gets a little more pronounced. But not bigger. Just more...present."

Emily paused. "Now I want you to send some gratitude to it. It showed up today to give you information. Can you just thank it for that? And when you do, notice if anything changes."

Jade's expression shifted. Something softened.

"It got a little smaller," she said quietly.

"Now we're going to hand it a microphone," Emily said. "Like a karaoke mic. Ask it: what have you got for me? It might be a word, a picture, a sentence. Just notice what floats through."

Silence.

Jade's brow tightened, then released. "It's saying...what if they look and just keep walking."

Emily was quiet for a moment. "Where did that come from? Your chest or your head?"

Jade paused. "My head," she said. A little reluctantly.

"That's what usually happens first," Emily said. "Your mind is fast. It's used to getting there before anyone else does." She paused. "Let's go back to the oval. Ask it again. Not the thought around it. The sensation itself."

Jade went still. She was trying.

"I'm not getting anything," she said.

"Stay with it," Emily said. "You don't have to produce anything. Just keep the line open."

More silence.

Then: "There's a girl."

Emily didn't move. "Tell me."

Jade exhaled slowly. "She's probably eight, maybe nine. Standing outside at recess, watching the other kids."

A pause.

"What's she doing?"

"Just watching," Jade said. "She wants to go over, but she's not sure they'll want her. So she stays at the edge."

Emily waited.

"What do you notice about her?"

Jade's voice went quieter. "She's trying to figure out what they want her to be. So they'll let her in."

"That makes sense," Emily said. "That was smart, actually. That strategy worked, probably. Kept her safe in a lot of rooms."

She studied Jade for a moment through the screen.

"But here's what I want to ask you." Her voice shifted slightly, direct but warm. "Have you ever stopped and appreciated that little girl? Not pitied her. Not felt sorry for her. Actually appreciated what she figured out how to do?"

Jade didn't answer right away.

"She became really good at reading people," she said slowly. "Like, really good. She could tell when a room shifted. What someone needed. What was safe to say."

"Yes," Emily said. "And who does that sound like now?"

Jade went still.

A long moment.

"Me," she said quietly. Like she was just now seeing it.

"She's the reason you know how to sit with a customer for an hour before you pick up a single stone." Emily paused. "She's not a wound to fix, Jade. She's where your work comes from."

Jade's breath released unevenly.

"Where did she learn it?" Emily asked. "That she might not be wanted."

Jade was very still. "My parents split when I was eight. My mother stopped wearing her ring. I found it in the back of her dresser drawer." She paused. "I asked her why she didn't wear it anymore. She said sometimes things change."

Emily held that.

"She learned love could be put away," Jade said quietly.

Jade's hand went to her ring.

"Yeah," Emily said. Just that.

Then something shifted in Jade's expression. Soft and sideways.

"I design jewelry," she said.

Emily waited.

"That's what I do. I help people find the right piece for the person they love. Engagement rings. Anniversaries. The necklace that says I see you." She shook her head, something between a laugh and a breath. "My core wound is I'm not lovable, and I've spent six years in the business of love tokens."

She looked at the screen. "You can't make that up."

"No," Emily said. "You can't." A pause. "And you're very good at it."

"I know," Jade said. Quietly. "That's what makes it lonely sometimes. I know exactly how to find the piece that says I love you. I just don't always know what to do when it comes back the other direction."

Emily held that.

"What does a kid do with that?" It wasn't really a question.

"She decides she must not be lovable enough to make it stay," Emily said. "So she gets really good at reading whether someone is safe before she'll let them in. She becomes the one doing the deciding. Not them." She paused. "The girl at recess. The customers you sit with for an hour. Fashion Week." She stopped. "It's the same question every time. Am I lovable enough for you to stay?"

Jade didn't say anything.

"I want you to hear something," Emily said. "People do business with people they know, trust, and like. Like is just love in a business context. It's the same thing with a different name." She paused. "And when you don't believe you're lovable, when part of you is always waiting for someone to decide you're not worth keeping, you can't fully let them in. You manage them instead. You sit with a customer for an hour, and you're brilliant, but there's a part of you standing at the edge of the room the whole time, watching to see if they're going to leave."

Jade was very still.

"They feel it," Emily said. "They can't always name it. But they feel it. And some do get through anyway. The ones who come back. Who bring their daughter. Who say you understood exactly what they meant." She paused. "When you let them in, you get to actually feel it. Not wonder if they're there for the jewelry. For you."

A long moment.

"Lovable isn't something they get to decide," Emily said quietly.

A silence.

"She's been waiting her whole life to hear you say she's lovable," Emily said. "Not for you to rescue her. Just to see her. To tell her she got it right, even if it cost something."

A long silence.

"What would you want to say to her?" Emily asked. "Not to fix it. Just to let her know you see what she built."

Jade was quiet for a moment. When she spoke, her voice was low.

"I'd tell her she didn't have to earn it. That she was lovable before she figured out how to read a room. Before she got good at anything." She paused. "That the things she thought made her strange are the things that make the work matter."

"And what does she do with that?"

Jade almost laughed, soft and surprised. "She doesn't totally believe me. But she's listening."

"That's enough," Emily said. "You don't have to convince her today. That old belief had years to take root. You've been running it so long you stopped noticing it was there. The new one needs the same thing: to hear itself out loud, more than once, until it takes hold. You don't plant a seed and walk away. You come back."

Emily let the silence hold for a moment.

"How's the oval feeling now?"

Jade checked in. "Still there. But it's not heavy anymore. It's more like...it's just resting."

"Good. That's what we want. Not gone. Just not running the show."

A pause.

"Here's your homework," Emily said. 'I am lovable.' Say it out loud. Every day. Before the sales, before the customers, before the rooms full of people." She paused. "And then notice what happens in your body when you say it. That's the only job. Not to feel it yet. Just to notice where it lands." Another pause. "As a choice. Because you decided. Before anyone else gets a vote."

"I am lovable," Jade said quietly. Like she was trying it on.

Emily let that sit.

"Some days it'll land," she said. "Some days the oval comes back. Either way, you come back too."

"That girl at recess. She doesn't need you to rescue her. She just needs you to stop leaving her at the edge. Every time you let someone in, you're telling her it's safe now. You don't have to convince yourself. You just have to let them come close."

Jade was quiet for a moment.

"Okay," she said. Simple. Not a big declaration. Just a yes.

"Good," Emily said. "I'll see you in the group."

The Story

Her brother called at the same time he always called. Early enough that she was still in the car, late enough that he figured she was done for the day.

"How was it?" He didn't specify what he meant. He never did. He always meant everything.

"Good." She looked at the steering wheel. "It was a lot, actually."

"Good a lot or bad a lot?"

"I'm not sure yet." She watched a woman cross the parking lot in front of her. "Somewhere in between."

He didn't push. It was one of the things she'd always counted on about him. He didn't require her to have the answer before she was ready.

He was quiet for a moment. Then: "You sound different."

"Different how?"

"Less on." A pause. "Is that okay?"

"Yeah," she said. "I think it's okay."

"The trunk show pieces looked amazing, by the way," he said. She could hear him in his kitchen, something on the stove. "I showed Mom the photos."

"You didn't have to do that."

"I wanted to." His voice was easy. "She said they were beautiful."

Jade didn't say anything.

"She did," he said, as if she'd argued.

"I know she did." She looked out the windshield. Her brother had always believed in her. She had once made a pair of earrings in her first year working with wire. They came out crooked.

He hadn't let her throw them away.

A pause.

"The session was about why I keep people at arm's length," she said. "Even the ones who've been standing right there the whole time."

"What did you figure out?"

"Apparently, my deepest wound is that I'm not lovable." She almost laughed. "Which is something, given that I've spent six years helping people find the piece to give to the person they love." She shook her head. "I've been in the love business this whole time. Just not the receiving end."

He was quiet.

"That tracks," he said. Careful. Not unkind.

"I'm right here, you know," he said. Quiet. Not pushing. Just saying it.

"I know." Something in her chest shifted. "You always have been."

He let that sit. Then: "What did you decide? About the show."

There it was. She'd known he would ask.

"I'm doing the boutique show," she said.

Silence. Not the comfortable kind.

"Jade."

"I know."

"Fashion Week. That's the room you've been talking about for two years."

"I know it is." Her voice was steady. Something in her was steady. "And I'll get there. Just not like this."

"What changed?"

She thought about the girl at the edge of the playground. About the oval in her chest going quiet.

"I'm not scared of it anymore," she said. "That's what changed. The session took that out of it."

He waited.

"So why the boutique show?"

"Because it's what I actually want." The words settled as she said them. "I want to find the person who doesn't know yet what they need. I want to sit with them and figure it out together. That's the work I love." She paused. "Fashion Week is about the room deciding you belong. The boutique show is about the work. I finally know which one is mine."

She hadn't known she was sure until she said it out loud.

"Those aren't the same thing," he said. Carefully.

"No," she agreed. "And I'm okay with that."

She could hear the stove clicking off.

"Okay," he said finally. The word landed differently than she expected. Not like he was convinced. Like he trusted her. "Tell me everything about the boutique show."

She sat in the car a few minutes after they hung up. She was thinking about those earrings. Crooked, lopsided, made with wire she hadn't known how to work yet. She had cried because they weren't right.

He had kept them. She found out years later that they were still in a box in his room, sitting next to a varsity pin and a birthday card from their grandmother.

She used to think that was just him being sentimental.

She thought she understood it now. He hadn't kept them because they were good. He kept them because he loved her. Not because the wire was right. Not because she'd earned it. Because she was his, and that had always been enough.

She'd been surrounded by it her whole life.

She was just learning how to let it in."I do everything here." She glanced back briefly. "It's mine."

"Tell me about one of them," Emily said. "One of the pieces you're working on."

Jade turned and looked at the workbench. "I'm making a set of earrings. Sterling. Very simple. The customer wants them to look like something her grandmother might have worn."

"What does that mean to you? Visually?"

"Small. Not fussy. But with weight to them. Like they know what they are."

"I like that. Like they know what they are." Emily looked at her. "How's business?"

Jade exhaled. "Good. Better than good. I have a trunk show in six weeks."

"That's significant. Where?"

"A gallery in the city. They reached out to me. I didn't go looking for it."

"How did that feel? When they reached out?"

Jade was quiet for a moment. "Honestly? I spent two days waiting for the other shoe to drop."

"What would the other shoe look like?"

"Them realizing they'd made a mistake."

"And did they?"

"No. They confirmed twice. Sent a contract." She looked at

her hands. "I signed it."

"Good. Let's look at your numbers." Emily pulled up the screen. "You scored yourself a six in the business domain. Tell me about that."

"I'm good at the work," Jade said. "I know I'm good at the work."

"And in the room with people? Selling it?"

"That's different."

"What's the difference, in your body, between those two?" Jade considered. "When I'm making something, I disappear into it. I'm just there. But in a room with a buyer or at a show, it's like..." She paused. "Like I'm performing being someone who deserves to be there."

"Performing." Emily held that. "Okay. I want to activate something. Can you close your eyes for a moment?"

Jade nodded and closed her eyes.

"I want you to imagine you're at the trunk show. It's the first morning. You've just set up your table. The room is starting to fill. A buyer walks toward you. Impeccably dressed. She looks serious. She picks up one of the earrings, the sterling ones we talked about, and she studies it for a long moment. Then she looks at you. What happens in your body right now, picturing that?"

A pause.

"There's something in my chest," Jade said.

"Okay. Where exactly?"

"Center. Sort of upper center."

"Stay with it. What is it doing? Is it pushing, pulling, tight, expanding?"

"Contracting," she said. "Like... bracing."

"Does it have a size?"

"Not large. About the size of my fist."

"Does it have a shape?"

"Round. Mostly."

"Is there a temperature to it?"

"Cool," she said. "Colder than the rest."

"Does it have a color? It may not."

Jade was quiet for a moment. "Something dark. Navy, maybe. Hard to say."

"Okay. I want you to zoom in on it. Like you're looking at a piece up close. Is there anything about the surface?"

A pause.

"Dense," she said. "Like wet clay."

"Does it have a temperature?"

"Cold."

"Okay. Stay with it. Don't try to make it go away. We're just observing it." Emily's voice was calm. "Does it change when you observe it?"

A longer pause.

"Slightly," Jade said. "Like it knows I'm there."

"Good. Now relax into it. Like a warm bath. Just let it be there without bracing. Does it get bigger, smaller, or stay the same?"

"Smaller," she said. "Just slightly."

"Good. Now feel some gratitude for it. I know that sounds strange." Emily's voice was easy, not performative. "This thing has been in your chest for a long time. It's been protecting you. Can you thank it for that?"

A long pause.

"Yes," Jade said finally.

"Does it change?"

"A little warmer." She said it with mild surprise.

"Good. Now we're going to hand it a microphone. We're going to turn it up and ask it what it's been protecting you from. Don't think. Just notice what comes."

Silence.

A long silence.

Emily waited.

"What's coming up?" Emily asked softly.

Jade exhaled slowly. "She's probably eight, maybe nine. Standing in the doorway of her parents' bedroom. They're fighting. Not loudly. That was somehow worse. Just cold and contained and like it had been going on a long time before she got there."

Emily held the space.

"I used to hide the things I made," Jade said. "I'd make things in my room and then put them away before anyone saw them." She paused. "Not because I was embarrassed. I didn't want anyone to touch them. They were mine. Nobody could say anything about them if they didn't know they existed."

"What happened to the things you made?" Emily asked quietly.

"My grandmother found them once. She was visiting. She looked at everything for a long time without saying anything. Then she said, 'These are beautiful. You made these?'" Jade's voice was even. "And then she said, 'Why are you hiding them?'"

Emily waited.

"She kept them," Jade said. "The ones I'd made. She asked if she could have them and I said yes." She touched her bracelet. "I didn't know until years later that she wore them."

"What does it feel like to say that out loud?" Emily asked.

"Like something easing," Jade said quietly.

Emily studied her for a moment. "What does it feel like when you show someone your work now? A stranger?"

"Like I'm handing them something real and hoping they handle it carefully."

"And when they don't?"

"Like I knew better than to hand it over."

"But you keep showing up." Emily's voice was direct. "That's not nothing. That's the whole thing, actually."

Jade looked at her hands.

"What's happening in your chest right now?" Emily asked. "The clay thing?"

Jade checked in. "Still there. But it's not heavy anymore. It's more like... present."

"Like it's listening."

"Yeah."

"Good. Here's what I want to name," Emily said. "You have been making things and protecting them your whole life. That's not a wound. That's a skill. You know how to tend to what's delicate. You know how to care for something before it's ready for the world." She paused. "The question is whether you can let people see the work while you're still in the room."

Jade was quiet.

"The belief underneath," Emily said. "The one we're working with today. The one your body just showed us. The other side: 'I am lovable' when it comes to stepping into a bigger stage. Being seen in a competitive room. Letting the work be judged by strangers." She looked at Jade carefully. "That's a lot to carry."

"It is," Jade said.

"Here's what I want you to do this week. Once a day, before you start any work, I want you to say out loud: 'I am lovable.' Not 'my work is good.' Not 'I deserve to be here.' Just that." Emily held her gaze. "And I want you to think about what it would mean to show up to that trunk show not as someone performing confidence, but as someone who makes beautiful

things and knows it."

Jade nodded slowly.

"One more thing," Emily said. "The ring you're wearing. Did you make it?"

Jade looked down. "Yes."

"Do you wear your own work often?"

"Not really."

"Why not?"

She was quiet for a moment. "I guess I never thought it was for me."

"Wear it this week," Emily said simply. "Every day. That's it."

The call ended.

Jade sat at the bench for a while without picking up her tools.

She looked at the ring.

She'd made it three years ago. A simple band with a small stacked detail that had taken her four attempts to get right. She'd

made it for a customer who changed her mind. She'd kept it because she didn't want to put it in the case.

She'd never thought about why.

The Story

Her grandfather had kept everything.

His garage was a study in organized accumulation: labeled boxes, sorted hardware, tools hung in traced outlines on pegboard. When he died, her father and uncles spent three weekends sorting through it all. They found fishing lures organized by size, spools of wire by gauge, coffee cans of sorted screws. They found a shoebox.

Inside were small objects: a button, a piece of ribbon, a faded photograph, a child's drawing on lined paper. And the things Jade had made. The rings and the small pendants and the one complicated brooch she'd built when she was eleven and thought it was terrible and had thrown it away.

He hadn't thrown it away.

He'd kept everything.

Her father handed her the shoebox at the funeral, matter-of-factly: "Grandpa would have wanted you to have these."

She had sat in her car for twenty minutes before she could drive.

She still had the box. She'd looked at those pieces recently and seen things she hadn't known she knew how to do yet.

Not

because the wire was right. Not because she'd earned it. Because

she was his, and that had always been enough.

She'd been surrounded by it her whole life.

She was just learning how to let it in.

CHAPTER 17

Every Seat

Theodore texted the day before to ask what time the performance started.

Roman almost asked how he knew about it, then remembered he had mentioned it. Three weeks ago, at the shop. Just in passing.

He texted back: 7pm. Parking is terrible.

Theodore replied: "I'll find it. We'll be there."

Roman and Laurie arrived early, the way Roman arrived everywhere. She had Andrew's name circled in the program before they found their seats in the second row of a school auditorium with folding chairs and a curtain slightly too long for the stage.

Theodore arrived at twenty minutes to seven. Marianne was beside him, still in her coat. Theodore found Roman and Laurie without difficulty and steered them both toward the second row.

"You made it," Laurie said.

"Of course," Theodore said.

He introduced Marianne. Roman shook her hand. They settled into the four seats, coats in laps, programs open.

"First time?" Theodore said.

"Yes." Roman looked at the program. "He was running lines in the car the whole way over."

Theodore kept his eyes on the curtain. "Wonder where he gets it."

Roman looked at him. Something close to a smirk.

The lights went down.

When Andrew came on, Roman almost didn't recognize him at first. It wasn't the costume. It was something in how he held himself. Upright and easy at the same time. He delivered his lines with a clarity that sounded nothing like the kid Roman drove to baseball practice twice a week.

He made them count.

Roman looked at the program again after Andrew's scene. He smoothed the corner with his thumb.

"He was good," Theodore said quietly.

"He was." Roman set the program on his knee. "I was more nervous than he was."

Theodore didn't respond. He watched the rest of the performance with the focused attention he brought to things he respected.

Afterward, in the lobby, Andrew found them. Still flushed, still in the energy of it, he stopped short when he saw Theodore and Marianne standing beside his parents.

Roman made the introductions. Andrew shook Theodore's hand, which surprised Roman.

"Did you come for the whole thing?" Andrew said.

"We did," Theodore said. He looked at the boy directly. "Most people forget to listen when they're not the one speaking. You didn't. That's the harder part."

Andrew stood a little straighter. He looked at his father, then back at Theodore. "Thank you," he said. He meant it.

They said their goodbyes outside. Theodore and Marianne's car was two rows over. He raised a hand in farewell without turning around.

Roman watched them go. Then he looked at Andrew beside him, still talking, already somewhere else in the story of the night.

His father had built the firm. Had worked eighty-hour weeks. Had never once, in Roman's memory, come to anything like this.

He didn't say any of that. He unlocked the car.

Laurie caught his eye over the roof. She smiled, small and knowing, the way she did when she didn't need to say it out loud.

Andrew was already in the backseat.

"I want more next time," he said.

Roman got in. He looked at Andrew in the rearview mirror. Andrew was still lit up, still in the energy of it.

"You lost a line up there," Roman said. "I saw it."

Andrew looked at him.

"You found it and kept going. You didn't wait to see if the room would fall apart." He paused. "Most people don't know how to do that yet." He started the car. "You already do."

Roman looked at him in the rearview mirror.

"Go get more," he said.

Every Seat

The room was the same. The long oak table. The water glasses at each place. The whiteboard wiped clean.

What was different was harder to name. They had arrived before Emily again, the way they always did now. No one had needed to find a seat. They just knew where they sat.

Emily came in from the hall, set her folder on the table, and looked at them for a moment before she pulled out her chair.

"Last one," she said.

Nobody argued with that. Nobody tried to make it smaller than it was.

She opened her notebook. "Tell me what's been different."

Julia went first.

"I signed the lease on the space next door." She looked at her mug. "I've been looking at it for eight months. Running the numbers. Running them again." She paused. "Last week I called my attorney, and then I just signed it." She set the mug down. "I didn't send it to anyone else first."

Cameron filed it the way she filed everything.

"I let Jake run the spring rotation." She looked at the table. "Start to finish. I didn't check his work once." A pause. "And I said yes to dinner."

"Both felt like the same thing, actually."

Theodore spoke without looking up at first.

"I called Evan." His thumb moved once to the edge of his watchband. "Gave him the go-ahead on the website."

He looked up briefly. That was all he needed to say about it.

Roman brought his eyes back from the window. He'd been watching the street.

"I sent the Ellison proposal." He said it the way you say a simple thing. "He called the same afternoon. We're meeting on Thursday." A pause. "I had the urge to run the numbers again before the meeting." He stopped. "I noticed it. I didn't."

Jade turned her ring once.

"I told my team we're not doing Fashion Week." She looked at the table. "We're doing the boutique show instead." A pause. "They weren't happy about it." She turned her ring. "I made the call anyway."

She didn't say anything else. The room understood.

Emily let it settle. She looked at each of them in turn.

"That's not the same group that sat down here three months ago," she said.

Nobody disagreed with that either.

Emily closed her notebook on the table. Not with finality. Just to change what her hands were doing.

"I want to ask you something different," she said. "Not about the decisions you made this week." She looked around the table. "About the people around you. What have you noticed?"

The room settled.

Julia said, "The bookkeeper called twice with questions." She looked at her mug. "My first thought both times was that I'd made a mistake somewhere." She stopped. "But I caught it faster than I used to. She just had questions." She paused. "I didn't spend the day looking for what I'd done wrong."

Cameron said, "Jake called it right. The rotation." She looked at the table. "The numbers came in before I'd even thought to check." A pause. "I didn't fix two things before I told him that."

Theodore spoke without looking up. "I called Evan. Gave him the go-ahead." His thumb moved once to the edge of his watchband. "He wasn't surprised. He'd been ready for a while." A pause. "I just hadn't noticed that before."

Roman had been looking at the window. He brought his eyes back. "I watched Andrew lose a line last night. He stopped. Then he found it and kept going." He paused. "I wasn't watching for the mistake. I was just watching him."

Jade turned her ring once. "My team's disappointed," she said. "I can feel it when I walk in the room." She paused. "I used to need to fix that."

Emily held the room.

"Here's what's happening," she said. She stood. "The work you've been doing on these beliefs doesn't just change what you think about yourself. It changes what you see when you look at other people." She paused. "Think about wearing sunglasses with scratches on the lenses. A tint. Everything you look at is colored and distorted. You adjust to it so gradually you stop noticing." She looked at the table. "When you're carrying the belief that you're not enough, or not worthy, or not valuable, that's the lens you're looking through. Every face becomes a potential verdict. Every room becomes a test." She paused. "As the beliefs start to move, the scratches clear. The tint lifts. The people around you stop being judges. They start just being people."

She let that land before she continued.

"Walk in convinced you're not worthy, and you find the evidence in every face. A quiet question from your bookkeeper sounds like doubt. A missed call sounds like rejection. The field manager who does it differently sounds like a verdict." She stopped. "As the beliefs clear, so do the reflections. The bookkeeper is just learning the job. The rotation Jake ran is just good farming. Your brother calling every week is just someone who loves you." She looked at the table. "The relationships don't change. What changes is what you can finally see in them."

She stopped.

"And it goes the other direction, too. When you're carrying the belief that you're not enough, you don't just find it in other people's faces. You send it out." She paused. "You hold the people around you to the same standard your inner critic holds you to. You don't mean to. But they feel it." She looked at the table. "Work on judging yourself less, and you'll find you judge everyone less. Believe you're enough, and you stop sending the people around you the message that they aren't."

Cameron said, "I've been micromanaging Jake because I didn't trust myself." She said it flat, like a fact she'd just confirmed. "It had nothing to do with him."

"No," Emily said. "It didn't."

She walked to the whiteboard. Picked up the marker.

"There's one more belief I want to name today. The last one in the assessment." She wrote it plainly.
I don't belong.

"This one is a little different," she said. "The others tend to color everything. They're a filter over the whole day." She paused. "This one is more specific. You can walk into a room this morning and feel completely at home. Different room this afternoon, and you're scanning every face, waiting for someone to notice you don't belong." She set the marker down. "Same belief. Same day. Different room."

She turned to the room.

"It sounds different from the rest. It's not about what you've done or what you have. It's about whether you have a right to be in the room at all."

She paused.

"You didn't write that. You absorbed it. From people doing what they could with what they had." She stopped. "It was never yours. You've just been carrying it."

Julia said quietly, "Without Marcus, I didn't know if I still had permission to be in the strategy half."

"Yes," Emily said. "He didn't take anything. But when he left, you didn't know if the permission left with him."

Theodore looked at his hands. "When my father stopped coming in," he said slowly, "it wasn't just that the work felt less valuable." He paused. "It felt like I was less allowed to be there."

"Yes," Emily said. "The room was still yours. But the permission felt like it walked out with him."

Cameron said, "I've been running a farm that was never supposed to be mine." She stopped. "For years I've been waiting for someone to come out to the field." She paused. "I don't even know what I was waiting for them to say."

Emily held that for a moment.

Jade said, "I kept waiting for someone in that industry to tell me my work was real." She paused. "Like the work couldn't be real until they said so."

"Yes," Emily said. "You were letting the room decide."

Roman was looking at the table. He already knew.

"Every time I ran the numbers again," he said, "I was asking someone."

"Yes," Emily said.

She let the room sit with it.

"What you did this week matters," Emily said. She looked at each of them. "Every one of those things. They are the belief moving."

She was quiet for a moment.

Emily stood.

"Think about a time you hosted a party," she said. "An after-hours, a dinner, didn't matter the size." She paused. "You wanted people to feel welcome. You watched the room. You introduced the person standing alone to someone they'd like. You made sure nobody's glass sat empty too long." She looked at the table. "Your energy was pointed outward the whole night. You weren't wondering if you belonged there. You already knew. You were the reason everyone else did."

She let that sit for a moment.

"Now think about the last time you walked into a networking event where you didn't know anyone." She paused. "New group. New room. You weren't sure you'd been invited to the right thing." She looked at them. "You scanned the faces. Wondered if anyone would talk to you. Held your drink a little tighter. Waited for someone to signal that you were supposed to be there."

Cameron let out a breath. It wasn't quite a laugh.

"Same person," Emily said. "Two completely different experiences of the same thing. Walking into a room."

She walked a step.

"When this belief is running, you walk in as a guest. Not sure you're supposed to be there. All your energy pointed inward." She paused. "As this belief clears, you walk in as the host. Already decided. Energy pointed outward. Not checking. Contributing." She paused. "That's what it looks like to belong to yourself. When you belong to yourself, the room stops getting to decide."

Roman said, "Offense instead of defense."

He wasn't asking. He was placing it.

"Yes," Emily said. "Exactly."

Nobody said anything.

"Before you walk into any room, a meeting, a negotiation, your own field, a dinner table, ask yourself: am I showing up as a guest or as a host?" She paused. "You get to decide. Every time."

She sat down. She was quiet for a moment.

"I was at an airport in Barcelona. End of a long trip. Nineteen days." She paused. "One rolling bag. One backpack. Everything I needed, nothing I didn't."

She looked at the window.

"A woman sat down across from me. She'd been on the same cruise. Nine days, seven ports." She paused. "She had a checked bag. A carry-on that barely made the weight limit. A backpack."

She let that sit.

"It had been that way the whole nine days. Getting on the cruise, she needed help. Every Uber, she was loading and unloading. She'd had to get to the airport early just to check the bag. Every transition cost her something extra." She paused. "She got where she was going. She always got there. But it required her attention the whole time."

She looked back at the table.

"We got talking. She looked at my bag and asked how I did it."

Emily was quiet for a moment.

"I told her I used to pack exactly like she did. Extra of everything. Something for every emergency I could imagine." She stopped. "She wasn't packing clothes. She was packing for everything she was afraid of." She looked at each of them. "I'd spent years doing the same thing."

Theodore had gone still. His hands were open on the notebook.

"What you've been doing in here isn't just changing a belief," Emily said. "It's learning what's actually yours to carry."

Roman was looking at the table. His hands had gone flat against it.

"You can put it down," Emily said. "Over and over, every time you notice you've picked it up again." She paused. "It doesn't end today."

She looked at each of them.

"Everything else, you already have."

Nobody moved.

Julia looked at her notebook. Cameron had gone still. Theodore's eyes were on the whiteboard.

Roman said, "Thank you." Quietly, to no one in particular.

Emily looked at him. "You did the work," she said. "All of you."

She looked at each of them once more. Not performing it. Just taking stock.

"Before you go, I want to put something on the table." She paused. "The work you've done here doesn't stay inside you. It shows up in your relationships. With the people you lead. Your families. The ones closest to you." She looked at each of them. "There's another round of this work, and that's where it goes. The beliefs that shape how you show up with other people." She stopped. "I'd like to take you there if you want to go." She paused. "You don't have to decide today. Just know the door is open."

They gathered their things. A few quiet words crossed the table. Theodore moved the extra notebooks to the end of the table, the unremarked habit he'd developed by session three and never stopped. Cameron said something to Julia that didn't carry.

Julia held the door.

Roman was the last one out. He stopped in the doorway and looked back at the room. The long oak table. The water glasses still half-full. The whiteboard.

Emily was erasing it.

He watched the words go.

Then he left.

After

The afternoon was cooler than it had been in the morning. They came out of the building one or two at a time.

Jade and Julia walked out together. At the edge of the lot, Julia said, "The boutique show."

Jade looked at her.

"Not Fashion Week." Julia paused. "That was the work."

Jade was quiet for a moment. "My team's not thrilled about it."

"No," Julia said. "They wouldn't be." She paused. "Still the right call."

Jade glanced at her. "You called your attorney, and then you just signed it."

"I did," Julia said.

They stood there for a moment, in the way of two people who recognize the same thing in each other and don't need to name it.

"Are you going to do the second round?" Jade asked.

Julia looked at the building. "I don't know yet." She paused. "Are you?"

Jade didn't answer right away. "I don't know either."

That felt honest enough for both of them.

Cameron was already at her truck. She had her hand on the door handle when Theodore passed behind her without turning.

He raised a hand.

"Hey," Cameron said.

He stopped.

"Nice work," she said. Just that.

He turned. He looked at her. Theodore didn't smile easily. He didn't now. But something in his face settled, the way a piece of timber settles into a joint that was cut for it.

"You too," he said.

Roman came out last. He sat in his car without starting it.

He thought about Andrew in the auditorium lobby. What Theodore had said to him. Most people forget to listen when they're not the one speaking. You didn't. That's the harder part.

He thought about the whiteboard.

He started the car.

Epilogue

Six weeks after the mastermind ended, Julia closed on the expansion lease. She started demolition the following Monday. She told no one about the demolition until the contractor was already there. She hadn't needed anyone to weigh in on it.

She stood in the doorway between the two spaces with a cup of coffee, watching the wall come down. The smell of the bakery moved through the gap as it opened. Butter and plaster dust and morning light.

She had what it took. She had known that for a while.

She stood there until the contractor asked her a question; she answered without hesitation, and they kept going.

• • •

The summer evenings had gotten quieter. Not because there was less to do but because Cameron let herself stop.

She was still first to the field most mornings. That part hadn't changed. But she was inside by seven most nights now, and when the porch light came on, she let herself sit.

Bruce started coming by on Tuesday and Thursday evenings, usually around eight. He'd come around the side of the house without knocking. Sometimes he brought something, sometimes he didn't, and they'd sit in the old chairs and watch the light go off the fields.

She hadn't told anyone about it yet. She wasn't sure what to call it. He didn't seem to need her to name it either.

One Thursday, he said, "Jake ran a good rotation."

"He did," she said.

That was most of it. The rest of the evening was just the fields and the sounds they made.

The yields came in above projection.

She texted Jake: *You called it right.*

He wrote back two hours later: *Thanks for letting me.*

She kept the text. She didn't know why. She just did.

•　•　•

Roman signed the Ellison agreement on a Thursday afternoon. He sat with the paperwork for ten minutes before he filed it.

He picked up Andrew from rehearsal on a Friday. Andrew came out of the building with his jacket half on, still talking to someone behind him, and jogged to the car.

He threw his bag in the back and then stopped.

"Can I drive?"

Roman looked at him. The permit was eleven days old. Roman had signed the form himself and still wasn't sure what he'd been thinking. Or what their state was thinking.

He thought about it for exactly as long as it deserved.

"Yeah," he said. He got out and handed over the keys.

Andrew adjusted the mirrors with the methodical care Roman recognized from somewhere. They needed to stop at the Caldwell site on the way home. Andrew pulled in without being asked, parked cleanly, and got out.

Roman had expected him to wait in the car.

He didn't. He walked the whole site. He stopped at the open framing and ran his hand along a stud. He looked up at the roof joists. He asked the site foreman what went in next, and when the foreman answered, he nodded like he was filing it away.

Roman watched him.

His son moved through a job site the way Roman had always wanted to, but never had. Curious without performing it. Interested in the thing itself. Not measuring himself against it.

Andrew drove. Roman watched the road from the passenger seat.

"Is that the big one?" Andrew said. "The one you talked about at dinner?"

"Ellison's different," Roman said. "It's a firm. Thirty years of clients. Twelve people." He paused. "You can't walk a firm."

Andrew thought about that. "Can I see the office sometime?"

Roman looked at him. "Yeah," he said. "You can."

Andrew nodded and kept his eyes on the road.

Roman watched the road go by from the passenger side.

He was still smiling when they pulled into the driveway.

•   •   •

The showcase ran on a Tuesday. Low light, long tables, twenty designers in a converted warehouse.

The first two hours were steady. Buyers moved through efficiently, took photos, and made notes. Most didn't linger.

In the third hour, a woman stopped at Jade's table without reaching for her phone.

She picked up a cuff. Turned it. Set it down and picked up a pendant instead. Gold. Simple. The kind of piece that didn't announce itself.

"What's your shop like?" Jade asked.

Buyers weren't usually asked questions. The woman looked up. "Small," she said. "Fifteen years in the same spot. We don't carry anything that needs explaining."

"Who comes in?"

The woman smiled a little. "Women who know what they want and don't want to be sold."

"Tell me about one of them," Jade said. "A regular."

The woman paused. Then she started talking.

She stayed for forty minutes. She placed an order before she left. At the table, she looked back at the pendant.

"My customers are going to ask about these."

"Good," Jade said. "Tell them to ask you. You'll know what to say."

The woman left. Jade sat alone at the table. The room had thinned out. Late afternoon. Light through the high windows onto the work she had brought.

She reached into her bag.

Her mother's ring was there. Plain gold band, worn smooth. Her mother had worn it every day of her marriage, and then one day hadn't. Jade had been carrying it with her for three weeks. Not putting it on. Not leaving it in the drawer either.

She held it for a moment in her palm.

Then she put it back.

Not yet. But it was somewhere she could reach it.

That was new.

•   •   •

The little wooden truck was on the kitchen table when she came in from outside.

She stopped in the doorway. She recognized it. She'd seen it once, years ago, when they were still young, and Theodore had shown it to her like it was something he wasn't sure he should show anyone. His dad had carved it for him when he was small. She hadn't held it. She hadn't asked to.

He was standing at the counter with his back to her, stirring something on the stove.

"Found it in a box in the back closet at the shop," he said, without turning around. "Dinner's almost ready."

She came in and set her gardening gloves on the counter. She looked at the truck. It was small enough to fit in a child's hand.

The paint was mostly gone. Then she looked at the table. He had set it. Both sides.

"He carved it himself," Theodore said.

"I know." She had known. He'd told her once, years ago. Once, was how Theodore told things.

She sat down. He brought the pot over and served her first, then himself, and sat across from her. They ate the way they used to eat, before. At the table. Together. Not in shifts.

After dinner, he found the remote.

"Want to watch the Wheel?" he asked.

She was already sitting down.

Marianne had the puzzle before the second letter came down. She always did. Theodore had known this about her for thirty-one years and had long since stopped trying to get there first. Mostly.

"R," he said.

"I already have it," she said.

He was watching her face more than the screen.

At the first commercial, he turned down the sound.

"Emily sent an email," he said. "Second round. Same group."

She looked at him.

"Are you going?" she asked.

He nodded once.

Something settled in her face. She looked back at the television.

"Good," she said.

The next puzzle came up.

She held off. Gave him time.

He took it.

"B," he said.

"There it is," she said.

"Next one," he said.

"Next one," she agreed.

The game show played on.

Closing

You made it.

I mean that. You sat with this story all the way through, and that tells me something about you. You didn't pick this book by accident.

Roman, Julia, Cameron, Theodore, and Jade. Five completely different lives. Five completely different invisible beliefs. And if you're honest with yourself right now, one of them feels a little too familiar. That's not a coincidence. That's the whole point.

Here's the thing about the beliefs we carry quietly. They don't show up in the boardroom labeled "I don't trust myself." They show up as a decision you second-guess for three days, a delegation you never quite make, a version of success that keeps moving just out of reach. They're subtle. They're smart. And they've been running longer than you've been a leader.

But you know they are there now. That changes things.

If you want to go deeper, the methodology behind this story lives in my second book, Traveling Light: Free Yourself From the Crap in Your Head. That's where the full framework lives. It's not a fable. It's a field guide. And if something in this story activated you, Traveling Light will give you the tools to do something about it.

If you want to keep this conversation going, I'd love to have you on my email list. That's where I share what I'm working through, what I'm seeing in my coaching work, and what's coming next. You can sign up at bfreakingawesome.com.

And if part of you is wondering, "Could this work for me? Not a character in a story. Me, specifically, in my actual life, with my actual business?" That's a real question and it deserves a real answer.

I work with a small number of executives and business owners at a time. The work is exactly what you watched Emily do with these five characters. It doesn't happen in one sitting. But it does happen, so the answer is yes.

If you're curious, reach out. You can find me at bfreakingawesome.com.

One more thing before you go.

I co-host the Be Freaking Awesome podcast with my daughter Sami Kinnison. Every week we talk about the real stuff. Leadership, mindset, business, and the kind of life that's worth showing up for. Come find us wherever you listen to podcasts. Just search Be Freaking Awesome.

I wrote this book because I kept watching brilliant, capable, genuinely good people hit walls that had nothing to do with skill or strategy. I wanted to write something that didn't explain the problem to death, but let you sit inside it and recognize yourself.

I hope it did that.

If something struck you, I want to know. Send me an email at [angela@angelabelford.com]. Not just to say you liked the book, though I never mind that. Tell me which character you saw yourself in. Tell me what shifted. Tell me what you're still sitting with.

Because this conversation doesn't end here.

The next book is already in the works. Stay close.

Until then, keep doing the work.

You are either green and growing, or dead and dying.

I vote green.

www.ingramcontent.com/pod-product-compliance
Lightning Source LLC
Chambersburg PA
CBHW051001060726
47593CB00018B/2010